THE MAGIC

OF

2 SECONDS

Make Better Decisions, Avoid Silly Mistakes and Become Self Aware

By Maxim Dsouza

Disclaimer:

Although the author has made every effort to ensure that the information in this book was correct at press time, the author does not assume and hereby disclaim any liability to any party for any loss, damage, or disruption caused by errors or omissions, whether such errors or omissions result from negligence, accident, or any other cause.

The information contained within this book is for educational and entertainment purposes only. No warranties of any kind are implied. The advice offered can have results different from what is mentioned. The readers acknowledge that the author is not engaging in the rendering of legal, financial, medical or professional   advice.

Table of contents

CHAPTER 1

The Instant Decisions That

Go Wrong

1 .....
2 .....

Two seconds just went by as you read that. Seemed lightning quick, didn't it? But are 2 seconds really that fast? At first glance, they seem too rapid to even notice. But if you think again, you will realize how things can go haywire in just an instant. Good things happen over a course of time, but silly mistakes and poor decisions occur instantaneously.

Do you remember an instance when you said something wrong and regretted it right after? I remember many such bloopers with my words. Before I go into my stories, let me bring up other noteworthy examples first.

The President of the United States is among the most powerful people in the world. His words echo around the globe and reach billions of people in an instant. The President has to make sure he says all the right things because not only does he lead his country but also operates as a worldwide figure.

Can you guess what's more critical for the President than saying the right words? It is making sure he does not say anything wrong. All Presidents carefully ponder about what they intend to say. Even when journalists ask them the trickiest questions, they maintain a calm head and provide a fitting reply. But are they perfect? Of course not. They are human, and they make errors too. I present to you some of the words Presidents have said which ended up as major bloopers.

A slip of the tongue:

When Barack Obama served as the President, he attended The Tonight Show With Jay Leno. Obama joked about his terrible bowling skills and how he practiced in the White House alley to improve his score. Obama said, "I bowled a 129," to which Leno replied, "That's very good, Mr. President." In an attempt to crack a joke, Obama said, "It's like the Special Olympics or something."

Oops, bummer! The President had unintentionally hurt the sentiments of the Special Olympics and the disabled people across the world. He received calls demanding an apology before the telecast even aired on TV. Obama went on to say sorry for the emotions he had hurt by not thinking his words through.

Here is how Bill Clinton made a mess. The National Geographic Society had placed a 500-year-old Incan Mummy on display in Washington. The mummy called "Ice Princess" was a 12-14-year old girl. Sources claim she was killed by a blow to her head and sacrificed to the Gods. At a fundraiser, Mr. Clinton said, "I don't know if you have seen that mummy. But if I were a single man, I might ask that mummy out. That's a good-looking mummy." Well, Mr. Clinton found that funny, but others didn't. Anthropologists and historians criticized the careless remarks of the President. Newspapers went on to ridicule his comments. A search on the internet will help you find those articles even today.

You can find many such mistakes made by other Presidents like George Bush, Richard Nixon, and Donald Trump. Pretty much every President has a story attached to his name where he said something he shouldn't have. Likewise, many celebrities have erred with their words too.

When a BBC reporter asked Dalai Lama for his thoughts on his successor being a woman, he replied, "I mean, if a female Dalai Lama come, then she must be very attractive. Otherwise not much use." No one knows whether he meant that or wanted to sound funny, but he sure did enrage women all over the world. He isn't the first well-known person to make a controversial statement, nor will he be the last. Many famous people often face ridicule for using the wrong words at the wrong time.

Momentary mistakes:

I will stop with the examples from celebrities because they have a media reporter lurking over their shoulder, waiting to pounce on a little mistake. Regular people like you and I make many such errors ourselves. Thankfully, our stupidity does not feature in the newspapers or turn into a meme on the internet. But we say the wrong things all the time. And are our instantaneous mistakes restricted to badly spoken words alone? Not at all. When we fail to think through, our actions and thoughts create even more damage than words.

Let's look at an event involving common people with no cameras or microphones. On May 10, 1996, about 33 climbers had set out on their dream to scale the Mount Everest. For challenging expeditions like these, individuals go through a professional mountaineering company who help them get to the summit. The climbers that day were from two different companies, Mountain Madness, led by Scott Fisher and Adventure Consultants led by Rob Hall.

Back in those years, scaling the Everest, an intimidating 8850m mountain, was one major goal mountain climbers had. For the companies, it was not just passion but also business. Each client paid roughly 50,000$ to reach the summit. So the pressure to succeed was immense and both the companies were on a mission to get their clients to the top. The leaders and the guides had years of experience in the dangerous snowy mountains. Rob Hall had climbed the Everest 5 times before. Scott Fisher had a tremendous record of scaling most of the toughest mountains around the world, including Everest. The leaders of both teams were among the best of the best.

The expedition began as usual where people expected a tough climb. One by one, they started facing delays that seemed small on their own. When the team had reached an altitude of 8,300m, the guides had not finished setting up the fixed ropes. An hour went by as everyone waited for the experts to complete their job. A few hours later, the climbers reached the final obstacle of the journey. Only a hundred feet away from the summit lies a 40ft rock wall called the Hillary Step, named after the first man to get to the summit, Sir Edmund Hillary. Both the teams faced further wait while the guides set up the path to get over the final barrier.

Since 33 climbers had to go through the same bottleneck, more time was lost. One of the guides reached the summit at 13:07, while the other climbers followed behind. As per the guidelines, the safe time to reach the summit is by 14:00. Any attempt to scale the Everest beyond that deadline can make the descend before dark too risky. Any chances taken can even be life-threatening. But on that day, many of the climbers had not reached the summit at 14:00. In the previous year, Rob Hall faced a similar delay and he decided to return without reaching the summit for the safety of the people. Lou

Kasischke, one of the climbers, mentions that, when Rob saw Scott going for the summit, he ignored the strict schedule. Both Scott and Rob knew the risks involved but decided to proceed.

Rob and a few others made it to the top with a minor delay of about 30 minutes, which for experts isn't too hard to handle. They began their descent at 15:00, but on their way back, Rob met one of his clients who was on his way up at the Hillary Step. Rob ordered him to turn back, but Doug was adamant about reaching the summit. After the convincing failed, Rob decided to help Doug reach the goal faster and started climbing up again to assist his client. Scott Fisher, the other leader, was falling ill by then but kept his climb going. He managed to reach the summit only by 15:45, while Doug and Rob reached even later. A 2-hour delay in a nasty mountain climbing expedition is nothing short of playing with your life.

When the descent began, the weather started worsening, adding more trouble to the already delayed quest. The blowing wind combined with the chilly snow added to the woes of the exhausted climbers. They had no choice but to slow down. But the weather had no mood of slowing down that night. By 18:00, the wind had turned into a full-fledged blizzard. Snow pricked at people's faces at 70mph, the visibility reduced, and the ropes tied during the ascent got buried under the ice, making the way back to camp impossible. The sherpas and the other guides tried their best to help the climbers reach back to safety. But the tenacity of the mountain and the ferocity of the weather had closed the doors for any rescue mission.

By the end of the expedition, eight climbers lost their lives, including both the leaders, Rob Hall and Scott Fisher. Some of the bodies were never recovered. Other mountaineers found Rob's body a few weeks later, but his wife asked them to leave it in the mountains because she believed he would've liked to stay there. The tragedy has left a scar in the mountaineering industry forever.

Several unforeseen factors played their part in the mishap. The bottlenecks at two points, the unexpected storm, the illness of people are among the few. None of these were under the control of Rob or Scott. But the expedition leaders had the choice of returning when they had overshot the deadline of 14:00. The decision to continue beyond 14:00 is considered one of the major reasons for the catastrophe.

Sitting here today, knowing what transpired, it is always easy to analyze a disaster in the hindsight and blame the people for it. Thinking straight and making the right decision is known to be hard at high altitudes due to the lack of oxygen in the body. All the mountaineers knew of the possible risks beforehand. Rob and Scott did their best to make the descent successful, so blaming them is beside the point. But, could a simple decision of turning back when they couldn't reach the summit by 14:00 saved people's lives? Yes, it would have. Given the circumstances, emotions, and business impact, it was not an easy decision, but in terms of analysis, it did not require more than a few seconds to make the judgment.

Such errors in judgment happen in various situations and it comes down to a quick decision that goes wrong. Hundreds of such stories exist today.

On April 14, 1994, two pilots of the US air force misidentified two friendly helicopters from the US State Army as Iraqi aircrafts. The pilots destroyed both the helicopters killing a total of 26 military and civilians on board.
Such a drastic attack required multiple confirmations. Many vital steps were missed before the pilots committed such a grave mistake. When one pilot misidentified the helicopter, the other failed to notify that he did not see the same. Other

personnel involved with the engagement assumed some other team member would have carried out the necessary safety and compliance checks. Many people failed in their responsibilities that day simply because they thought "he" or "she" must have done it already. A simple confirmation from any one person involved might have prevented the shoot down.

Situational mistakes:

In a panic situation, impulsive decisions are quite common. In any sport, you will notice referees behaving differently during the tense moments. During the grand final of a championship event, referees go gentle due to the fear of making a poor decision. NBA statistics show that 50% fewer fouls are called during the last minutes of an intense game.

Sometimes, errors occur due to haste and lack of verification. In 2005, a stock trader at Mizuho Securities, Japan wanted to sell one share for 610,000 yen, which translates roughly to $5,500. Unfortunately, he failed to notice that he had erroneously reversed the figures. Instead of selling 1 share for 610,000 yen, he sold 610,000 shares for 1 yen. Though the firm gave their blood and sweat to cancel the order, their efforts failed. When the day ended, Mizuho Securities had lost $225 million. The error sent a ripple down the entire Japanese stock market. A costly mistake committed in a matter of seconds.

Different events have different reasons. The Everest disaster occurred because the experts overshot safety deadlines. The Black Hawk shootdown happened due to various people failing their basic checks. Referees are surrounded by the pressure of a million fans. The stock market error was triggered by haste, lack of verification, and poor administrative processes.

The importance of little decisions:

You and I may not make decisions that cost lives or lead to dire consequences. The stories mentioned were to highlight the importance of a few seconds in decision making. Maybe, our circumstances are simpler but that does not rule out an area for improvement. We make poor decisions all the time, many of which can be avoided. While each of them seems minor in itself, they bottle up like a volcano. The day it explodes, it creates a huge mess. Some of the common errors in judgment we make are:

- Starting an argument
- Hurting a loved one
- Procrastinating a task
- Deciding to waste another hour on Netflix
- Eating 500 unnecessary calories
- Taking a needless risk

When you hear the word "decision," you think about a significant step in life, like a career change or buying a house. But 99.9% of the decisions you make are far simpler daily activities like snoozing the alarm, picking the outfit for the day, skipping your workout, replying to uncomfortable questions, and more. The big decisions like moving to a new city, getting married, having kids, investing a large sum of money, or buying a house occur once in a blue moon in comparison. When you're emotionally charged or intoxicated, avoiding poor decisions can turn challenging. But, the 2-second principle does not intend to make you perfect. Even if you manage to steer away from a few of your mistakes, you still win.

The Magic Of 2 Seconds

In real life, you make way more small decisions than big. Therefore, due to the difference in numbers, the mistakes you often make are simple. Take for example, munching on a pizza and gulping down a can of soda. You do not realize the impact of your decision when you bite on the last crumb or finish the last sip. You feel the pinch when you stand in front of the mirror topless, and your belly pops out. "If only I had not eaten so much junk," you curse yourself. The interesting part lies in how you forget the mistake as soon as you stop feeling the damage of your poor decision. The moment you put clothes on and your tummy is less apparent, you move on. A few hours later, you order a burger for lunch, because, well, who cares?

You want to do something. You do it. You regret the decision. You forget what happened. You repeat it.

This turns into an endless cycle.

Make no mistake, the loop does not apply to eating or speaking alone. It applies to many other aspects of your life like:

- Making a hasty decision
- Violating a good habit
- Slipping back to a bad habit
- Postponing things for later
- Wasting time idling

The examples can go on and on. Sure, you feel bad about what you did, but you never think about preventing yourself from making the same mistake again. Since the error seems small, you shrug it off and move on. You go on a hunt for big changes or ideas which can lead you to success. You worry more about the occasional major decisions in life and choose to ignore the other 99.9%.

Think about it from a different lens. What if you could avoid those silly mistakes? What if you could prevent the nasty remarks you make accidentally? What if you could prevent yourself from eating junk every time you felt like? What if you could avoid buying things you don't need? What if you could stick to a good habit without going astray time and again?

This book will try to teach you to avoid such errors. This is not a foolproof method to stop all your silly mistakes, but it can help you prevent many of your little missteps. Using the 2-second principle, you can learn how to be more mindful of the small decisions you otherwise make without any thought. Please note that the technique will not help you come up with a billion-dollar idea. It will only prevent you from getting punched in the face or shooting yourself in the foot.

The book is all about improving your smaller decisions in life by thinking quickly in just 2 seconds. So let's get right to it.

CHAPTER 2

The 2 Second Principle Explained

I can feel you staring at the book with disbelief. If I were around you, you would ask me, "Wait a minute. Did you just say better decisions in 2 seconds? I barely move my butt off my couch that fast."

Yes, I do hear you. 2 seconds seem too short to make any significant difference. But they are too quick only when you look at the time taken to perform an action. When it comes to processing a thought, 2 seconds are plenty.

Take a real-life example. The phone rings, and you hear the voice of your good friend on the other side. You have no clue whatsoever about the topic he will talk about. Yet, words pour from your mouth, and you have a conversation that flows like a river.

Do you have to think hard to reply? Not usually. Are there pauses in between? Only sometimes.

Your brain can process what your friend said and come up with a response within a fraction of a second. To top that, you don't need any conscious effort either. Isn't your brain fascinating? It sure is. So stop underestimating what your mind can achieve in 2 seconds. It can do an astounding lot. This book will teach you how to use your brain in those 2 seconds to make a better decision.

Before we get there, let's talk about how your body reacts to the world around you. Your normal flow of actions in the absence of the 2-second principle follows this pattern:

- Receive
- Act
- Regret

You receive information from your senses. For example, you might see something interesting that makes your eyes sparkle, hear words that make your blood boil, or encounter a new opportunity that flares your chest.

Triggered by what you receive, you spring into action. You might scream abusive words or get ready for a fistfight. I am not only talking about cases of anger. When you hear a piece of exciting news, you dance in public without enough thought. You simply do what you feel like without thinking it through.

When your emotions diffuse soon after, it's too late already. You already have paved the path for some damage by making a wrong decision, hurting relationships, or making a fool of yourself. The sequence ends with you regretting the consequences you have to face.

Let us break down each of these three steps one by one:

Receive:

As a human being, your body never stops receiving information. Your five senses, namely eyes, ears, nose, tongue, and skin, help you accumulate information. They exist to trigger a response from your brain based on what you receive. Some of your senses, like the ears or skin, are active even when you're sleeping. Let's look at some examples for each of the senses and how they prompt a reaction.

- Eyes - Watching your favorite soccer team score a goal makes you scream
- Ears - A nasty comment from a coworker makes you verbally retaliate
- Nose - The odor of burnt food makes you sprint to turn off the stove
- Tongue - The taste of a bitter dish makes you cringe
- Skin - The feeling of a tiny little creature crawling in your shirt makes you jump and brush it off

In addition to these five senses, thoughts can also trigger your actions. Thought doesn't fall under the category of human senses as per science though.

Take a moment to recall all the stupid things you have done before, big or small.
- Uttered something miserable to your crush? You were blinded by the good looks.
- Fought with a friend? His joke got on your nerves.
- Gobbled down a burger with double patty and dripping cheese? Your nose gave in to the aroma while passing by the restaurant.

You receive information and react right after. You only need a split second to hear, feel, or see something before you respond. But sometimes, you might receive information from your senses for an extended period before you react. For example, your friend keeps making one nasty joke after another before you confront him. The aroma of food from a nearby restaurant hits your nostrils for an hour before you decide to buy the dish. Your senses can set off a reaction immediately or after a while. More often than not, your action occurs instantly after receiving the information.

React:

Your action is the second part of how events transpire. Based on what you receive, you think, speak or perform an action. Sometimes you do the right thing. Sometimes you goof up. Sometimes you have no clue whether what you did was right or wrong. Your actions can include a wide range of activities which are too many to list. I will list down a few for reference:

- Showing your awful dance moves to a bar full of people because your best friend challenged you when you were drunk
- Buying those trendy clothes even when your credit card was overdue
- Justifying your opinion with reasons when someone disagrees with you

Don't cover your face and hide in the corner if you have done such things before. If it makes you feel any better, I have committed similar foolish mistakes which I wish could go back on a time machine and erase. Unfortunately, I don't own such a device and my bloopers will continue to embarrass me for the rest of my life.

Regret:

After receiving and reacting, follows a period of regret. Regret or guilt follows every lousy action of yours sooner or later. Sometimes the grief is short-lived, sometimes it lingers on and on. It can last anywhere from a few seconds to weeks, months, or years. Interestingly you can calculate the duration of regret based on a real life mathematical formula.

Duration of regret = Stupidity of your action x No. Of people who know about it x Your shame factor

The regret of a slip of the tongue can diffuse in a few hours. But if you can dance drunk in front of all your coworkers, the guilt can last for a long time. The shame factor is a value specific to every person which determines how sensitive, emotional, and shameless you are. The higher the value, the more delicate your feelings are.

Let's calculate some values:

You tell your dad something you shouldn't have:
- The stupidity of your action = 4/10
- No. Of people who know about it = 2
- Your shame factor = 4/10 (not very sensitive)

Duration of regret for this case = 4*2*4 = 32
32 is not a value in time, like hours or days. It is only a number you can use to compare.

Let's compare that to dancing drunk in front of all your coworkers:
- The stupidity of your action = 8/10
- No of people who know about it = 35
- Your shame factor = 4/10

Duration of regret for this case = 8*35*4 = 1120

Now, do you see why you would regret tipsy dancing in public much longer?

One positive from the formula is that your shame factor isn't a constant. The more stupid things you do, the less shame you feel. It can come close to nil but never hit a 0. You will feel lesser regret with repeated foolish acts, but you will never develop a sense of complete shamelessness. By the way, do not start doing senseless acts to reduce your shame factor. That is not the message I am trying to convey. Moreover, the formula is just for fun, so relax.

What is the 2-second principle?

The 2-second principle is all about breaking the usual sequence of events by adding a simple step in between. To apply the principle, you must change the flow as follows:

Receive -> React -> Regret
To
Receive -> Pause -> React

That's how easy the rule is as per theory. You must allow your brain to make a better decision by waiting for an extra second or two before taking any action.

The Pause:

The only difference the 2-second principle introduces is a pause. The receive step remains as is because you cannot change what your senses collect. You can block certain information from reaching you, like turning off your phone, but the vast majority of what you receive lies out of your control. A coworker will make a sarcastic comment, an impatient driver will honk for no reason, and your friend will embarrass himself in public. You cannot control or change what your senses gather. You can only change how you react to what you receive. The 2-second principle helps you improve your actions using a pause of 1 second.

The Magic Of 2 Seconds

Are you raising your eyebrows already asking, "Only 1 second? What should I do during that second?" I am glad you asked. After the first step of receiving, you must use the next second to be more mindful of your action. I will present various real-life scenarios and provide examples of how you can utilize the pause to the best effect.

Among the different possible things to do during the pause, some of the most common options are:

1. Wait/Do Nothing

In some cases, using the pause to wait serves you the best. Let's say you're at a party and having a good time. Someone who isn't exactly your friend walks up to you, exchanges a few pleasantries, and makes a snide remark saying, "Hey mate, I heard your girlfriend dumped you. What happened?" Every party has one such fellow who believes he has the right to talk anything about anyone. I am sure you will feel a rush of blood in your veins about a random person asking an unnecessary question about your personal life. At that point, you have two choices:

A. Hit back with a comment:
You can show the person his place by saying, "Yeah, things did not work out between us, but that was better than being single forever like you are." You might manage to shut him up but more follows immediately or some other day. He makes a nasty comment, and you make a counter statement. By participating in such an unpleasant exchange of words, not only do you make yourself uncomfortable, but also those around you. Besides, if the comment turns into a banter of arguments, you spoil the happy feeling you were experiencing.

21

Unfortunately, your natural reaction to such scenarios is to retaliate. As human beings, you and I like to put up a defense. Whenever your ego takes a beating, your instinct will trigger you to fight back. Your brain tells you, "Wait a minute. Don't take that insult. Slap one back right at his face", as you mentally clench your fists and take the stance of Mike Tyson ready to begin the first round of boxing. Okay, I understand you will not turn physically aggressive, but if we could punch mentally, some of us would box all day long.

B. Do nothing:

Your second choice is to let it go. You can use a second to gather your thoughts and answer, "Yes, things did not work out between us, and I prefer not to talk about it." Yes, You will feel a tinge of discomfort about the comment made. You will also feel a prick for not retaliating. But you will save yourself any further unpleasantries. Until you make a habit of maintaining your composure to think straight, you will need the pause to ensure you do not instigate an argument, debate, or a fight.

I am not saying you must turn into a doormat for people to trample upon. Many a time, a harsh reply helps prevent further unsolicited comments because some people are major jerks who deserve a taste of their own medicine. Even those around you will applaud within their heads as a token of appreciation for giving the brute a reality check. "I am glad you did that," they tell you later while your shoulders relax.

Waiting does not mean you do nothing at all. Instead, while you wait, you must use the extra second to choose the right reaction. The pause will help your brain make a better choice. If you wait and still feel like hitting back at the other person, feel free to do so.

2. Ask yourself a question

The best way to harness the power of the pause is to use the time to ask yourself a question. Now the question you ask depends entirely on the circumstance and your personality. Though there are no right or wrong questions, this book will cover the kind of questions I ask myself when faced with different situations.

"How can I think of the right question? That too in 1 second? That's impossible for me," I can hear you complaining already. Let me remind you how powerful your brain is. You already ask yourself questions all the time. When your boss asks you to stay back for two more hours on a Friday evening, your vocal cords want to scream, "You may not have a social life, but I do." As much as you want to say such words, you ask yourself a question, "What would my words lead to?" You know very well that your remarks won't end up well for your future. So your scream turns into a muffled down, "Okay, I will."

Your brain asks itself a question, finds an answer, and makes a decision in split seconds that you do not even realize it happened. Your mind has learned to kick in during the right time and avoid disastrous consequences. When you start practicing the 2-second principle, you must ask yourself questions on all possible occasions to validate your response. Your intended actions do not always have to be as stupid as getting into a dispute. Even during less severe circumstances, you can validate your actions with questions.

For example, when you step inside your house, and you're about to throw the key somewhere, you can ask yourself, "What could happen if I did not place the key in the usual place?" You will hear an answer, "When I am about to leave the next time, I won't know where to find them." Boom, you just saved yourself the trouble of scampering around to find your keys the next morning. Asking such questions is easy because they're based on common sense, and you already have the answers to most of them. All you need to do is cultivate a habit of asking yourself questions. That's precisely what the pause will help you do.

3. Check for a mental bias

Our brain handles the process of making the right decisions throughout the day. It helps us drive on the right path to work, be kind to people, eat at the right time, and avoid bumping into a pillar. But what if I told you your brain could make biased decisions? What if your mind favors certain things and often compels you to make decisions that cause more damage than good? You will find that hard to believe.

Let us take a typical real-life case. You are sitting on the couch, munching on a bowl of popcorn and sipping on a coke, finding ways to kill time. You pull out your phone and head on to Amazon. Your homepage shows a portable Bluetooth speaker at a 66% discount. The page indicates that the deal ends in the next 19 hours.

What did your mind tell you? Unless you already are an electronics geek who knows the average price of such goods, you will consider that an attractive deal. You made the decision in a matter of a few seconds. Your mind told you, "Hey, the offer saves you 66%, and you have to decide in the next few hours. Should we buy the speaker?" Your brain convinced you that the deal was fantastic.

Whether you buy the speakers or not is irrelevant. Didn't your mind easily captivate you about the benefits of the offer, because you noticed a 66% discount? But, if you search for Bluetooth speakers on Amazon, you will find many others at the same price. But when your mind saw the first speaker at a 66% discount, it decided in a split second that the deal was a bargain. Your brain failed to consider how much a Bluetooth speaker costs on an average, what quality parameters to look at or if you even need one. You made the decision solely because your brain believes "Any item on discount helps you save money."

Do you believe you won't fall for discounts because you know that trick already? Guess what? Most people choose a discounted item even if they know the idea behind discounts. Studies made on online food orders have shown how customers opt for a dish or a restaurant offering a discount even if cheaper options are available. When you notice a discount, you do not check the other options enough to make a comparison because you believe you're getting a bargain.

By the way, your mind did not fool you on purpose but only replayed your beliefs. It processed all the information you had and made the best decision based on available data. The discount made you vulnerable to the anchoring bias, and the 19-hour deadline hit you with a scarcity effect. These are only 2 of the many biases the human mind is susceptible to. These biases will stick to your brain like algae stick to damp areas. No matter how much you practice, you can't clean them up thoroughly. Do you think you can get rid of the fear-induced in your body when you come face to face with a lion? No way. You might argue, what about the circus trainer? Sure, he might not fear the lion in the circus. Try putting him face to face with a lion in the jungle. You'll have your answer.

Building awareness of such flaws of the mind is the most you can do. You will not have success if you try to get rid of them. Aim to reduce the damage of such biases by knowing how they influence you. If you are unaware of such biases, you won't even know when you're making a poor decision. Once you're aware of the flaws of your brain, you can use the pause to check for a mental bias.

Why do you call this the 2-second principle instead of the 3-second principle?

I know the principle explains three steps - Receive, Pause, and React. While I could call it the 3-second principle assuming one second for each, I do not consider the Receive as part of the flow because you cannot control what your senses gather. You can, however, choose to pause and decide your response. Therefore, if I consider a second to pause and another to react, all you need is 2 seconds. Feel free to call it the 3-second principle if that connects with you better. As far as the method helps you make better decisions, any name works.

Why does a second make such a big difference?

Imagine you're driving back home after you've had a bad day. You're moving in jam-packed traffic waiting to get home. Just when it is your turn to go, somebody cuts you off forcing you to get stuck again at the red light. You fume with anger and yell out loud. You feel your body temperature soar while you honk and bang the steering wheel. Even after the driver has left, you are still emotional, and alert as a hawk, watching left and right to check if anyone will cut ahead of you again.

Such an impulsive response is called the Amygdala Hijack, a term coined by Daniel Goleman in 1996. It describes an emotional response that is immediate, overwhelming, and uncharacteristic due to a threat. Before we get to the reason behind such abrupt reactions, let's tap into the science behind the human brain, which is said to have three parts.

The gray matter you have today is a result of millions of years of evolution. Therefore, some parts of our age-old ancestors persist and help us survive. Let me elaborate on each of the three parts.

The Reptilian Brain: Lying at the lowermost part of your skull is the oldest portion, also called the brain stem. The brain carried this part even before humans evolved. It is primitive and plays a central role in controlling balance, temperature regulation, and breathing. It focuses on survival and responds by instinct or stimuli. This part of the brain operates as the primary component for reptiles even today. Have you seen a snake react to the slightest noise or touch? Now you know why.

The Limbic/Mammalian Brain: Located one layer above the reptilian brain is the mammalian brain. Not only does it govern short-term memory and the body's response to danger, but it also controls all of our emotions. It functions as the emotional center and decides whether you respond with flight, fright, or freeze. Being slightly primitive, it's primary focus is survival too, but emotions such as anger, frustration, happiness, and love also arise from this part.

Neocortex: This part of the brain is most evolved in human beings. All the intelligent things you can do which other animals cannot, arise from the neocortex. Without this clever little piece of the brain, no human would ever be able to solve a mathematical problem, plan the construction of a building, or even think of path-breaking ideas that changed humankind. It is responsible for many other aspects which set us apart from other animals, such as social interaction, language, and the invention of machines. In simple words, neocortex helps you with all your intelligent moves.

In a standard scenario, the sensory thalamus, a part of the reptilian brain, handles the stimuli first, passes control to the advanced neocortex leading to the right response. But, in case of an emotional or dangerous situation, the brain uses a different sequence to speed up the response. The neocortex is bypassed, and a particular part of the brain, called the amygdala takes over. The amygdala, located in the Reptilian Brain, only knows to react instantly without using any rational thought. Since the neocortex was bypassed, the part of the brain which handles reasoning never comes into the picture. As soon as neocortex starts reacting, you realize that you overreacted.

The brain does not always have the time to think and act for every little action. For example, if you spot a snake next to your feet while walking, you jump immediately. You do not spend 2 seconds thinking, "Oh, I see a snake. It might be poisonous, and I will be in danger if it bites me. I need to run." Instead, you react within the blink of an eye. This flight or fight response, which nature has ingrained in our body, helps us stay alive. You will notice animals, birds, and insects exhibit the same behavior when threatened.

The problem is, the same behavior pops up when you face a simple situation that threatens your comfort, for example, someone cutting you off or making a rude comment. Unfortunately, nature does not help you make the right decision in every single situation. It senses danger and asks the amygdala to react as soon as possible.

The brain takes about 6 seconds to diffuse the chemicals causing the amygdala hijack. But for the little decisions, your mind comes to its senses much sooner. One second can do wonders for your decision-making ability. The amygdala hijack occurs when you're under a severe threat physically or emotionally. But, in real life, circumstances aren't usually so threatening.

For example, you might feel like pouncing on a donut even though you stuffed yourself with hundreds of calories from a pizza. Will the sugar-filled calories of a frosted chocolate donut kill you? Of course not, at least not today. But adding more calories is detrimental to your health, and you know it. Since such decisions do not threaten you, your body won't enter a fight or flight response. Therefore, you do not need those many seconds to help your brain think clearly.

All you need to do is, pause and let your brain work it's magic for you. That's all the 2-second principle is about. The rule isn't sophisticated to explain the science any further. You can start applying it right away. Well, it takes some practice to make the most of your pause. But, once you get the hang of stopping for a moment, it becomes second nature.

The future chapters will cover various aspects of your life where you can pause to avoid silly mistakes and make better decisions. You will read about first-hand examples of applying the 2-second principle to improve your good deeds and cut down your poor actions and habits.

CHAPTER 3

The debates that no one wins trophies for

As human beings, we love to argue and prove our point. If each argument was followed by a prize ceremony, every medal manufacturer would be minting money.

A couple of years back, I was sitting with a bunch of friends. We met quite often back then, and each person knew the rest for a few years or more. The topic started with a casual talk about what's going on with each other's lives. Glasses clinked, and everyone said cheers. As the night went on, the conversation had steered in a different direction. We were on a mission to solve all sorts of random issues of the world. Thanks to the alcohol, our local gathering now seemed like an imperative meeting of the United Nations.

One topic which always creeps into drunken conversations and sparks up a debate is politics. People in every social group have their point of view, and our circle was no different. The controversy that night began with a recent event about a politician. Of course, the famous leader had a bunch of followers who went gaga over every little thing he did. And with such following also comes hatred. A good chunk of people in the room hated the politician.

If you observe, you will notice a peculiar reason why people loathe a celebrity. The logic applies not only to politicians but also to other areas, such as sportsmen, actors, singers, or businessmen. If you ask the question, "Why do you hate person X?" many people will shrug and mention, "I do not hate him, I hate his fans."

Likewise, some haters in the room were due to the extremism of the fans. Though the friendship between people was strong, we had a sense of rivalry on specific topics without exchanging words. This strife was about to pop up in full gear that night. As an hour passed by, the casual hi hellos turned into a heated argument. The supporters of the leader sang praises about every decision and improvement made. The other group had counter-arguments and found a way to belittle every point made. After another couple of hours had elapsed, a few people were fuming as they hurled abuses at each other. Thankfully no one flung any glasses. But another day, another time, another group and another drink, anything could have happened.

After all kinds of discomfort in the room, the debate came to an end. The next day when people came to their senses, a few amusing outcomes occurred. Some people did not want to look at each other in the eye due to words uttered the previous night. Some others had left early to avoid the embarrassment of facing the person they fought with. A few others managed to have an awkward conversation stating their debate was uncalled for.

If you look back, what good came out of a debate over politics?

Did either group change their opinion? Absolutely not. The followers remained staunch supporters of their leader while the other side still hated him from the deepest point of their intestine.

Did anyone win some brownie points from the politician for their fanatic support? No. The politician had no clue whatsoever about the mad debate that happened in a room somewhere miles away. Even if he did, he would not give a rats ass about it.

Did anyone win a trophy for their excellent debating and arguing skills? If anger, guilt, and shame qualify as prizes, many medals were distributed that night. Barring that, no one won any actual rewards. Most people exited the place asking themselves, "What a mess? How do we get things back to normal? Won't the other person remember the remark I made? Arrgh!"

The debate over politics was only an example. Friends argue about personal remarks, unnecessary jokes, past relationships, and anything under the sun. Who made a more persuasive argument is irrelevant because conflicts impact relationships either way.

The aftermath of debates

We debate over things that bring no good to anyone. The human ego is like a bouncing pad. Throw something at it, and it will hit back. To make that worse, you realize the consequences of your words and actions only after the situation is over. You debate and argue because your brain likes to stick to its beliefs. Your beliefs aren't restricted to religion, philosophies, and approaches to life alone. Your support for a sports team or your sense of fashion is also one of your own convictions.

When someone challenges your belief, the He-man(or the Wonderwoman) in you wakes up. He might have been lazy for a month, unwilling to show any energy when there was an actual need. But when your belief is under question, the superhero within you draws a sword to attack and holds a shield for defense.

The normal flow of events during an argument is

The first nasty comment - The trigger
Your defense with a reply - The retaliation
Back and forth exchanges - The battle
The end of the battle - Agree to disagree with anger
Regret/hatred/embarrassment

Why do we argue?

The human ego needs some stroking all the time. Don't you feel your cheeks turning pink when you receive a compliment? Doesn't your chest flare an extra 10 inches while you step up on the stage to receive a trophy? That's because, you like to feel superior and valued. But, when someone makes a remark against you and presents a belief that you disagree with, your body heats up. Disagreement appears like disrespect to your brain. You want to hit back. You want to prove yourself right. You want to make yourself feel superior again. And what is the easiest way to do that? You argue.

But are all arguments wrong? Not at all. If we had to categorize arguments, we could put them under two brackets.

Constructive arguments:

These are the kind of debates where the participants are trying to reach a better outcome. The common signs of a constructive argument are:

- Average or slightly high tone of voice
- Minimal movement of legs, hands, and fists

- People listening to each other and processing good ideas
- The discussion moving towards a conclusion

The last point is the most noticeable difference between the two types. Though people exchange views and disagree, the overall conversation moves towards an outcome which people agree upon. Not everyone is pleased about the final decision, but no one trades any punches or bad feelings.

Some examples of constructive arguments are:

- A group of friends deciding which movie to watch
- The co-founders of a startup discussing ideas to increase sales
- A husband and wife discussing ways to save money for their future

The prime ingredient for a constructive argument is an open mind where none of the participants are extremists about a particular side. Both parties are looking to reach a reasonable decision even if it involves a compromise.

Destructive arguments:

These are the kind of debates where the participants are hell-bent on winning the contest. The common signs of destructive arguments are:

- High to ultra-high tone of voice with screaming
- Hands up in the air, fingers pointing at others, clenched fists, raised shoulders and flared chests
- Each side eager to reply and attack instead of processing the points made
- A never-ending loop of made-up facts and figures where the involved parties don't reach a conclusion

The common reasons why destructive arguments occur are:

- The participant wants to prove a point at any cost
- The participant has a personal grudge against the others involved
- The participant has an unusually high ego
- The participant wants revenge for some prior event
- The participant has tolerated similar event/s in the past and cannot take it anymore

Some examples of destructive arguments are:

- Why one sports team is better than the other
- The causes for the failure of a project
- Husband and wife talking about spending quality time with each other

The reason why arguments turn destructive is, one side does not want to keep an open mind. The other party might try to reason out with logic and maintain a calm head, but soon things cross a line. When one side goes aggressive and illogical, the other decides to retaliate. After a point, both sides have lost sanity and go on to prove their point and disprove the other.

Destructive arguments are less about the topic at hand and more about the people and the emotions involved. If you're arguing for a long time and going in circles, you aren't giving a damn about the topic anymore. You are fighting for your ego, not to reach a logical conclusion. Such arguments end up with a pyrrhic victory, where no matter who wins, both sides have something to lose. The damage comes in the form of broken jaws, mangled egos, bruised emotions, and crippled relationships.

How can you avoid destructive comments:

You can use the 2-second principle to avoid unnecessary debates. If you spend a moment to pause, you can stop many quarrels before they even occur. You may not always be able to watch your words and actions when your emotions are running loose, but you will curtail the ones of small or medium intensity. To avoid a fight, we will use the approach of asking yourself a question.

When you pause, ask yourself questions like:

- How would my comment sound to the other person? Does it come across as offensive?
- Is it necessary to counter-attack? Does anyone gain anything by the exchange of words?
- How will the others around me perceive my argument?
- Is it necessary that the other side agrees with my belief or decision?

You must ask these questions before you start an argument. That's when you're emotions are just kicking up. After you have begun arguing, these questions create less of an impact. That's because by then, you have stopped caring about how you sound to the other person. Let me go through each of these questions in detail one by one.

How would my comment sound to the other person?

When you frame a response in your head, you only think from your mind. You don't know how it sounds in real life. Take for example, uttering, "I have told you many times before," to a friend of yours. From your perspective, you feel you're justified in making that remark because you have mentioned the same thing before. Turn the table around and imagine how would the same comment sound if you were the receiver. Wouldn't that seem like a complaint? Well, it depends on the tone of voice and context as well, but you will realize when your words sound offensive if you think as the receiver. If you ask yourself how your statement would come across, your mind can figure it out in a split second. It won't even need the one-second pause.

Is it necessary to counter-attack? Does anyone gain anything by the exchange of words?

Let us take the example where someone makes a remark you didn't like. Before you hit back, ask yourself, if any good comes out of your retaliation. Chances are your reply leads to a series of comments and remarks. Sure, you might have a better argument, but what's the point of winning if it spoils your mood anyway? Don't argue to disagree. Argue only if it adds value. The sweet smell of victory boosts your ego for a while but puts you into a stressful mindset. Many a time, remaining silent serves as the best way to prevent further damage. As an alternative, you can even joke about the comment made. The other person will have a tough time persisting with a follow-up remark because you're not fighting back. It is like boxing against a wall.

Again, you must gauge the situation, the context, the person, and other factors. You do not have to tolerate all snide remarks just to avoid fights. If someone has a habit of picking on people, giving it back may be the right thing to do. You can choose to respond in kind, in silence, or with a joke. Whichever option you pick, make sure you think your decision through instead of reacting on impulse.

How will others around me perceive my argument?

If you're in a group, your words do not remain constrained within the people speaking alone. Imagine you are with a bunch of coworkers at a dinner event. You receive a reward for a job well done, and a jealous colleague takes a dig at you. If you choose to snap back, your reply has more impact than the few words exchanged. Those around you will judge you for what you said, irrespective of how uncalled your colleague's comment was. The situation ends with the whole group gossiping, "Both of them were at fault." Take into account how others around will perceive your comment before you make one. A brief thought can help you zip your mouth and avoid unnecessary consequences.

Is it necessary that the other side agrees with my belief or decision?

In an argument, people feel the need to declare a winner. Take for example, the atheists vs. The God-fearing. Atheists never understand why people believe in God when science proves otherwise. On the other hand, a believer will ask an atheist to explain the reason behind the big bang. An atheist wants to shake the faith of the believer, and the devout person wants to sway the skeptic into believing in God.

Another example is the way introverts and extroverts enjoy life. The extroverts try to make their introvert friends socialize and speak more. They fail to decipher how anyone can enjoy an entire weekend at home. Introverts wonder how someone can go out for breakfast, lunch, and dinner with different groups without draining themselves out.

Each group tries to convince the other side of their thought process. For what? Why do you need to change the opinion of another person in the first place? Are you trying to convince the person to change or only trying to prove your point? In most cases, it is the latter. You cannot sway an atheist towards

38

praying every day or an introvert into partying every weekend. If you're trying such an impossible feat, it implies you are only trying to prove your belief and making the other person uncomfortable.

No matter how hard you try to change the other person's opinion, the chances that you will succeed are close to none. All that comes out of such persuasion attempts are offensive remarks, bitter sentiments, or silent complaints. Two sides can take opposite sides of an argument but still be right in their own way. Do not try to find a winner where there is no need to. When you encounter such a situation, tell yourself, "I agree to disagree." Ask yourself if there is a need to change the opinion of the other person. In most arguments, there isn't one.

Avoiding arguments helps you avoid unnecessary mental stress at that moment and the consequences that follow. All you need is two seconds to prevent a careless sentence from turning into a full-fledged war of arguments.

Arguments are just one of our bad habits. You and I have far worse habits which we wish we could avoid. In the next chapter, we will talk about our behavior of choosing easier immediate rewards which cost us in the long run. And again, we will harness the power of 2 seconds to avoid such mistakes whenever possible.

Current Chapter in short

- The aftermath of debates
- Constructive and destructive arguments
- How can you avoid destructive comments by asking yourself:
    - How would my comment sound to the other person? Does it come across as offensive?

- Is it necessary to counter-attack? Does anyone gain anything by the exchange of words?
- How will the others around me perceive my argument?
- Is it necessary that the other side agrees with my belief or decision?

CHAPTER 4

The joy of the present and the regret after

That night was a special gathering among a large bunch of friends. I was having a gala time at the party. One of our close buddies was moving to a different country. After a few drinks, the music invited everyone to the dancing floor to show their moves. That's the day I realized why bars do not have mirrors. If they did, people would notice how terrible their dancing skills are and head back to their seats.

Anyway, after enjoying a great night, the waiter arrived to check on us for the last order. Most of us lifted our palm to indicate we had enough for the night. But every group has one person who is never done drinking. Someone screamed, "Two shots of Tequila each, and we call it a night." Fast forward 12 hours later, I was holding my head which was burning from a terrible headache. "If only I did not give in to the momentary joy of the two little glasses of alcohol," I cursed myself.

I thought I had learned from the experience, but two weeks later, I gave in to momentary pleasure again. I was taking a walk back home after I had finished my workout for the day. On the way, I strolled past an ice-cream store. As I glanced at the menu, the picture of Death By Chocolate with all the melting sauces caught my eye. The sweet tooth in me applied the brakes and I stopped on my tracks. "Maybe I should get one. Let me take a look," my mind convinced me. In no time, I swiped my card and walked away with a bowl of over 500 calories.

What just happened? Why did I give in when I knew very well that eating so many calories of sugar was a terrible idea? Though the action seemed different compared to the Tequila shots, the reason I gave in was the same. The last time I had the excuse that my brain cells were impaired by the alcohol, but this time I had no reason. I had fallen victim to the phenomenon of instant gratification.

What is instant gratification?

Instant gratification is the tendency to opt for immediate pleasure instead of a better return in the future. You feel like you want something and you want it now. Right now! For the same reason, it is also called immediate gratification.
Even though you know patience and discipline will yield a better reward, you cannot resist the urge to indulge in immediate bliss. "Damn it," you say soon after. The most common examples of instant gratification occur with food, shopping, sex, and entertainment. The opposite effect, called delayed gratification, is when you put off a reward for a superior benefit in the future. You know what the better reward is, so when you manage to hold yourself back, you have delayed your gratification. Almost always, waiting for a better reward is a wiser choice.

Experiments and Research Conducted

Around the year 1970, Walter Mischel, a professor at Stanford University, conducted an experiment that is today well known as the Marshmallow Test. He chose children between the age of 3.5 and 5.5, gathered them together, and put them through an experiment. Each child was taken into a separate room and given one marshmallow. If he could resist the urge for 15 minutes without eating it, he would get another one. If the child ate the marshmallow within 15 minutes, he would not receive the second reward. After explaining the rule, the researcher would then leave the child alone in a room.

The children displayed frustration as they waited clenching their jaws. They made up songs, hit their heads against the table, pounded the floor with their feet, played with their clothes, prayed to God, and whatnot. Many gave up and ate the marshmallow. Experimenters also performed other variations of the test using a different reward system. About 10 years later, in the follow-up studies conducted on the same children, some fantastic results appeared. There was a correlation between the children who delayed their gratification by waiting 15 minutes and their academic competence. Further studies in 1990 showed the same children correlated with higher SAT scores.

But, do we need an experiment to prove the benefit of patience? You already know patience brings greater rewards, don't you?

Why do we go for the immediate reward?

Instant gratification syndrome stems from multiple reasons. You will exhibit such behavior due to one or a combination of the following.

1. Part of human evolution

During the early human period, survival was the primary area of focus. If one could not protect himself from predators, hunt food to eat or find shelter from the weather, the chances of death would increase. Surviving back then was all about immediate rewards. Today, that equation has changed. You have all your basic needs for survival, but your brain still has some leftovers from the primitive lifestyle.

2. Uncertainty

When you have to wait to receive a reward, an element of doubt creeps into your brain. "Will my efforts pay off, or is this all for nothing?" If you work at a job you hate, the uncertainty around starting your own venture brings a thousand questions to your mind. "What if my idea fails?" "What if I go bankrupt?" "Isn't it a better idea to stick to the salary I already get?" Since a delayed reward seems distant and uncertain, you choose to stick to a smaller reward which is immediate and certain.

3. State of mind

Your state of mind has a massive influence on the little decisions you make. When you're stressed, you might give in and light up a cigarette. Late evening, after a tough workout, your willpower would have grown thin. You might succumb to the temptation of chocolate brownie topped with the crunchy nuts and the mouth-watering sauce. In a joyous mood, you feel like spending some extra money to celebrate instead of saving. Your emotions can alter your thought patterns causing you to give in to instant gratification.

4. Greed and desire

As human beings, we want more. When you earn a promotion to the role of a Manager, you aim to become a Director. Once you make a million, you dream about 10 million. After you lose weight from a state of obesity, you strive for six-pack abs. Your goals keep getting tougher and tougher as you achieve them. While you chase these goals, the delay in receiving the reward seems boring. You want to reach your next milestone as soon as possible, so you try taking a shortcut for pleasure.

10 Examples of Instant Gratification in daily life

You give in to instant gratification in daily life whether you realize it or not. Here are examples to help you introspect yourself.

1. Wasting time on social media

Browsing the news feed of Instagram, checking pictures of what your friends are up to, liking beautiful photos, and posting stories on what you had for lunch seems fun. But you know that you are only wasting time by using social media unless you intend to become an influencer. The effect is more prominent in Millennials who have grown up in an era of the internet. You are well aware that you can instead use the time for something more productive. Yet, the current happy feeling urges you to keep scrolling.

2. Snoozing

Each morning you plan to wake up early and do the task which you have forever postponed. But when the alarm rings, you hit the snooze button without any further thought. All plans go out the window. The comfort of extra sleep outweighs the plan that gives you joy in the future.

3. Eating junk

You know you have to lose weight. You would feel more energetic, clothes would fit you better, and you would appear more desirable to the opposite sex. Yet, when you go to a restaurant, the juicy burger with a thick patty and melting cheese, sways your mind in the opposite direction. You give in and postpone your weight loss plans for the next week.

4. Skipping workout

When the clock shows 7 AM, and you know you must get ready to head to the gym, a thought creeps in. "What difference does it make if I skip one day? I will workout tomorrow without fail." Boom, your plans for a healthy lifestyle just took a U-turn. The comfort of laziness today overpowers the future benefits of a lean body.

5. Working on urgent tasks

When you are at work, an email that popped up catches your attention. You were taking a course on improving your skills, but the mail screams, "Open me, open me. I have some work for you which isn't urgent. But I know you want to check it now." The daily tasks take precedence over the long term goals you plan to achieve.

6. Spending time on entertainment

You have to do your laundry and stock up groceries for the week. If you do not, you will have to spend the whole next week ordering food online with your dirty clothes on. But what do you choose? You decide to open Netflix and watch one episode of the series you just started. When the show ends, one part of your brain says, "ok, let's wind up." The other part says, "Wait, hold on. We still have time." In the meantime, 10 seconds have elapsed, and Netflix has already started playing the other video.

7. Spending money instead of saving

You plan to save more money each month instead of blowing all your income on buying things you want. When your salary hits your bank account, you vow not to spend it all. But somehow, you face an "expected expenditure" which derails your plan. At least that is what you convince yourself. What's funny is, such accidental expenses occur every month. If you make up your mind, you can reduce the number of times you dine at restaurants or refrain from hitting the buy button on an item you peeked through on Amazon. But no, you don't feel like doing that, do you? You enjoy spending on what you feel like.

8. Paying a loan to buy a fancy item

You apply for a loan to buy an expensive asset which you cannot afford with your current income. Buying a house on a mortgage isn't a bad idea because the cost of the establishment shoots up over time. But not all of what you buy using a loan appreciates over time. For example, you buy a brand new car on a higher mortgage when you could have opted for a cheaper one. You justify your decision saying a reasonable vehicle is a necessity. But if your income increased by 30%, you would buy a car which is at least 30% more expensive by paying a high monthly installment. Your income increases, but your savings remain where they are. Have you ever analyzed what you're stepping into with a mortgage? You borrow money with a promise to repay with interest for the money you don't even have. How absurd is that?

9. Discount sales

When Amazon announces a big billion sale, you stand on your toes, waiting for the day to arrive. When it does, you scroll through the deals and add one item after another to your cart. You hit the buy button and rest back on your chair, smiling about saving a hundred dollars due to the discount. If you check your orders, you will notice that you don't need most of the items there. You will glance at some of those for a few days and toss them into a cupboard. The pleasure of buying something for yourself on sale gives you the instant gratification over saving money. A better decision was not to buy the item at all, but that ship has sailed now.

10. Alcohol/smoking/drugs

Addictions trigger a dopamine rush within your body. These are hormones secreted by your brain which makes you feel good. For the same reason, a drag off a cigarette seems like a stress buster. A pint of beer elates your mood. While all the addictions alter your state of mind in some way, the dopamine creates the craving to indulge in them again. Even though you know smoking and alcohol harm your health in the long run, you choose to relish them at the moment.

How to curb the action caused by instant gratification

Charles Duhigg, in his book, The Power of Habit, explains how each habit has a triggering point. Walking past a smoking area makes you pick a cigarette and light it up. Opening Amazon on your phone creates a temptation to buy something you don't really need. Sitting on the couch prompts you to open Netflix and spend the next few hours lazing around. All your habits have a triggering point associated with instant gratification.

Here is how you can use the 2-second principle to prevent the stupid decisions you make for such momentary rewards. You will have to apply both the waiting technique and ask a question method based on the situation.

The wait/do nothing technique

When you are trying to avoid a bad habit, waiting can solve the problem. Many of the choices you make are because you want to feel good at the moment. But give it a little time, and you no longer feel the same anymore.

- Waiting for a few minutes is known to overcome smoking pangs
- Postponing the decision to eat potato wafers can help you cut 200 calories
- Waiting for 24 hours will stop you from buying those new earphones from Amazon

Agreed that the wait is longer than 2 seconds sometimes. But when you find yourself making an impulsive decision for an immediate reward, use the pause to remind yourself to wait just a little bit more.

The ask a question method

You can ask yourself a question to make smarter decisions and avoid instant gratification. Some of the useful questions for such scenarios are:

Do I need this or want this?

You make all of your impulse decisions based on wants. You want to eat junk food, you don't need to. You want that new shiny watch, you don't need it. It might seem like asking yourself a question you already know the answer to. But when you ask yourself, you will notice your mind entering a self-realization mode which is coupled with guilt. Ask yourself, "Do I really need these new clothes I am about to order?." You might guilt-trip yourself and avoid the wrong decision. Sure, deep down in your heart, you knew you did not "need" extra clothes before you began looking. But when you pop the question in your mind, you will find it hard to lie to yourself.

Will the good feeling pass shortly?

You can apply the waiting technique differently. Instead of commanding yourself to wait, you can ask yourself if the joy that comes out of the decision will pass shortly. When you are about to indulge in a delicious looking burger, ask yourself, "Will I feel delighted a few minutes after munching the double patty and the dripping cheese?" You know you wouldn't.

I am not saying you should never order a burger. There are days when you badly crave for one, and there are some other occasions where you eat one just for the heck of it. Asking yourself the question will help you avoid the extra calories on the days where you eat a burger for no good reason. Many of the instant gratifications fall under the same umbrella. Sometimes you choose something because of your wants, but more often, it is purely based on habit. Examples include:

- Smoking during a break
- Browsing through the Instagram newsfeed
- Purchasing new clothes because you went to a mall

If you use the pause to speak sense into yourself, you can avoid impulsive decisions that stem out of nowhere.

Instant gratification is easy to fall victim to and not quite easy to fight against. Using the 2-second principle, you can triumph over some situations you would otherwise have given in to. The rule does not intend to throw instant gratification out the window. No matter what techniques you use, you will find the satan within you urging you to relish immediate pleasure. You do not have to turn perfect in 2 seconds. You only have to be better than you are right now by avoiding some of your missteps.

The Magic Of 2 Seconds

In the next chapter, you will learn about the human tendency to give ourselves rewards we do not deserve. The 2-second principle will help you overcome the bias in your head and make you reward yourself proportionate to your effort.

Current Chapter in short

- The pleasure of enjoying the present
- What is instant gratification and how it tempts you
- The reasons we fall victim to the effect - Evolution, Greed, Uncertainty, and State of Mind
- Different examples of instant gratification in daily life
- How to use two methods to fight the effect
    - The waiting technique
    - The ask a question technique
    - Do I deserve this?
    - Will the feeling pass shortly?

References:

Charles Duhigg. "The habit loop : how habits work." In The power of habit: why we do what we do and how to change. London: Random House, 2013.

CHAPTER 5

I can take that risk. Damn it, I shouldn't have

A few years back, I fired an employee for poor performance. He did a decent job on half his tasks but ignored the other half altogether. My solution to the problem was finding another employee who could do it right. So I did. It turned out that he was even worse. He couldn't even get half the things right.

"Where are all the good employees?" I said, slamming my fist on the table. After trying three different people for the role, I had my moment of enlightenment. None of the three employees were poor performers. My expectations were simply too high for one person to deliver. I was under the false impression that hiring another employee would solve my problem.

How do you react when you encounter a problem in your path? Does a thought flash in your head saying, "I can choose an alternative instead of dealing with this trouble right now." You must have heard the famous saying, "A known devil is better than an unknown angel." It implies you feel comfortable with a known situation or a person with flaws, even if you have a better alternative that you know little about.

But often, we tend to do the exact opposite of what the saying suggests. I have noticed myself and others around me choose an alternative we know nothing about instead of dealing with the problem at hand. I call this flaw of the mind as Alternative Option Paradox or Another Choice Syndrome. It is the gut feeling that another option might lead to a better outcome.

That's precisely what I did by hiring new employees one after another. I knew nothing about the next candidate I would employ. Yet, I believed he could do a better job than the current employee. I found a solution in an alternative instead of digging for the root cause.

Taking risks on impulse

Let me take a more straightforward example. Many employees are frustrated with their job and want to get out of it. Since they have heard about people in business making tons of money, they believe starting a business venture will lead to success. People feel like typing their resignation letter and embarking on their journey to riches. Quite often, you take the chance too, even if you do not know much about entrepreneurship.

Once you have taken the plunge, you realize that making a business successful is far more challenging than a regular job. Your lack of knowledge leads you to believe that any alternative is better than your current situation. I am not saying you must pick a regular job over entrepreneurship. But irrespective of what your current obstacle is, the alternative seems like a better choice.

Why do you fall victim to another choice syndrome?

1. Your brain thinks that the other option doesn't have any problems. Since you hardly know about the alternative, you aren't aware of the issues you might encounter. Your ignorance makes you more optimistic.

2. You compare the problems of your current situation with the benefits of the alternative. But that isn't a fair comparison.

To make the right choice, you have to compare the pros and cons of each side. However, your mind chooses a simpler task of looking at the current bad vs. The possible good. Besides, you are utterly ignorant about the negatives of the alternative. You realize the challenges only once you have stepped into the water yourself.

Here are some more examples of the phenomenon:

1. Investing money

You hear about people making tons of money by investing in the stock market. You try understanding the tactics of investing the Warren Buffet way. As time passes by, you break your head trying to understand the techniques of smart investing. When you hit a roadblock or incur losses, you spot an alternative investment opportunity that appears more lucrative. For example, you believe you could make money with ease in real estate instead. Even if you have never purchased a property before, you brim with confidence assuming whatever you buy will appreciate over the years.

2. A new potential partner

If you're dealing with trouble in your relationship, you might be attracted to a new person you just met. Have you noticed that when you walk with a bunch of people who are shorter than you, you appear 3-4 inches taller? Likewise, the flaws in your current relationship can make a jerk seem like a hero. You fail to consider that the new partner might have other imperfections that are yet to unfold.

3. Taking bigger risks

The alternative option paradox can influence you to take bigger risks than you usually would. The size and frequency of the chances you take depend on your risk-taking appetite. You will find two such tendencies - risk-taking and the risk-averse. You cannot categorize a person into one of these buckets because your decisions are situational. We will discuss that later in the chapter, but for simplicity of the concept, let us split people into two groups for now.

The risk-loving folks are like a cheetah waiting to pounce on its prey. They are always on the lookout for opportunities to grab. Three factors drive their decisions:

1. FOMO(Fear of Missing Out)

Every opportunity looks like a gold mine to them. If they let an opportunity pass by, they fear missing out on money, fame, success, or whatever they are chasing.

2. Taking all possible risks for victory

They are triggered by the success stories of people who took risks. They aim to achieve massive fame and loads of money by taking a leap of faith. No doubt, success requires the audacity to take a few chances. But sometimes the risk-loving people push it too far by taking a shot at a near-impossible target.

3. Making a decision now

In the hunt for success, the risk-loving people make quick decisions hoping for huge returns. Some of these decisions are hasty. They intend to hop on early into the bandwagon to reap as many rewards as possible.

The risk-averse people are the exact reverse. They have an allergic reaction to uncertainty. The risk-averse stay away from risks due to 3 primary factors:

1. Fear of failure

Whenever a risk-averse person has to take a chance, his mind gets paralyzed with the fear of things going wrong. "What if I lose what I already have?" echoes through his brain more than, "What if this risk changes my life for good?" His mind fights a battle between the benefits and the problems. He visualizes issues as an army of cavalry, infantry, and archers. The benefits, however, take the size of a small set of foot soldiers. The mental battle within the head of the risk-averse person is always won by the problems.

2. Losing what you already have

As per psychology, the grief of losing far outweighs the pleasure of winning. Such a tendency is called loss aversion, and various studies have proven this. As per the research, the pain you feel when you lose a 100$ is far more than the joy of gaining a 100$. Studies also state that the grief of a loss is 2-3 times the pleasure of winning. The most noticeable difference between the risk-averse and risk-loving lies in their loss aversion tendency. The risk-averse cannot overcome the fear of losing what they already have. The risk-loving do not like it either, but they take a chance believing in the prospect of a better return.

3. Afraid of stepping outside the comfort zone

Every risk involves some form of additional effort which isn't very comfortable. You may need to invest money, learn new skills, or do what you have never done before. The risk-averse people prefer sticking to their current comfort, happy with what they currently have. They do not intend to take a bet for better possible returns.

Now, I am not saying that one approach is better than the other. Being risk-loving or risk-averse comes with its own set of pros and cons. I am not asking the risk-loving people to take fewer risks or the risk-averse to take a leap of faith. But here's the kicker. A risk-averse person does not fear risks in all aspects of life. Similarly, a risk-loving person does not take a leap of faith with every single decision. Your appetite for risks depends on the task at hand.

I have a high risk appetite for business ventures and investments. But I cannot muster the guts to participate in adventures involving heights. The same can work in reverse. A person might hike the most dangerous mountains in the world as if he is walking in the park. But the same person might tremble at the thought of investing his money in high-risk stocks.

Your risk-taking appetite depends on:

- Your expertise in the task
- Your duration of experience with the task
- Your past stories of failures or success with the task
- Your reason behind doing the task(most important)

A person with a goal of covering all the world's best adventure spots has a purpose to bungee jump. I don't. I have a reason to make risky business investments because of my career and financial goals. The adventure traveler doesn't.

The decisions you make and the risks you take depend on the reason why you're doing what you're doing. If your why isn't strong enough, you will lean towards the risk-averse side.

When you have a compelling purpose, you'll take your chances with the risk. Try to look at yourself to validate the theory. You will find yourself bold enough to take risks in certain areas and taking the safer route in some other aspects. Everyone has a risk-loving and risk-averse side within themselves.

How to use the 2-second principle to take smarter risks

Knowing your risk-taking tendency for the current situation is the first step to making better decisions. As mentioned earlier, loving or hating risks has little to do with your personality and more with the circumstances. Identify if you're feeling risk-loving or risk-averse for that situation. If you are risk-averse, you can use the pause to check for pessimism. If you are risk-loving, you can pause to check for unrealistic optimism.

When you feel like taking a risk

You can use both the waiting and ask a question technique to make smarter moves and avoid unnecessary risks.

1. Wait

When you find yourself making a decision that involves a high amount of risk, simply pause and do nothing. The gap between the action and decision can diffuse the emotions involved. If you are in a casino, eager to place another bet, pause and wait. After the dice is rolled, you might not feel the same for the next round. When you're in a mood for taking risks, you crave for action. You feel your brain itching when you do nothing, which prompts you to make risky decisions. Postponing the action is the best way to help you avoid such a response in the first place.

2. Ask yourself if the reward is based on your assumption

Often, you assume you will receive a reward for your action. The problem is, you do not have the slightest breeze of evidence to support your belief. It directly stems from your mind because you believe so. You might even make up some fake evidence to validate your claims. In psychology, such behavior is called the confirmation bias. It is the tendency to only look at the proof that matches your belief and ignore facts that contradict your assumption. When we encounter evidence against our opinion, we reject them as exceptions or invalid. We love to stick to our opinion. We love to stroke our ego. We love to be right. You do so unconsciously without realizing the effect of the bias.

You may assume you don't make such mistakes, but we all are daily victims of the bias. Surprised? Let me give you an example. Do you support a political party? Most people do. How do you react when your party does a good deed which helps the citizens? You laud and praise them. How do you react when your party goofs up? You tell yourself, "they are human, mistakes happen," and shrug it off.

How do you react when the opposition party makes a mistake? You would complain, saying the party is good for nothing. When they do something good, you ignore it. You might even find a fault in their excellent work and go around telling people that the move was not as noteworthy as the world thinks.

The bottom line – you want your original belief to stay intact. If any information matches your opinion, you accept it. If you find any contradicting information, you either find fault with it or ignore it as a one-off case. Sometimes, opposing facts gets you emotionally charged up too. You even argue to prove your

59

point. Remember the fight you had with a friend due to a political belief, a sports team, or your preferred choice? You fell victim to the confirmation bias.

Whenever you assume any reward for your action, ask yourself if your decision is due to your assumption. You do not always have to look for concrete proof because that would lead to a risk-averse behavior. But use the pause to check if you are taking a blind leap of faith. Do you want to send an email to your boss saying "I quit" so that you can start your venture? Ask yourself if you have the skills to begin your venture. Waiting for a few months doing market research and developing your entrepreneurial skills could serve you better.

3. Ask yourself what the guarantee is

You can ask the previous question in a different form. Instead of asking if the reward is based on your assumption, ask yourself what the guarantee of the reward is. The modified version helps you make better decisions if you are eager for the prize. If you hate your current company and want to switch, ask yourself what is the guarantee that you will end up in a better place? What if the new company has a manager who makes your life miserable? Would you prefer finding a solution to your current problem, or would you risk an uncertain reward? When you ask yourself the question, your logical brain starts questioning the choice. In a second, you will avoid some of the bad decisions you would have made under impulse.

When you feel risk-averse

4. Ask yourself if you have considered the cost of inaction

When you feel risk-averse, your brain starts hunting for things that could go wrong with the action.

- Want to quit your job and start a venture? - What if my business fails and I lose my current comfort?
- Want to invest in mutual funds? - What if the market crashes tomorrow?

With a risk-averse mindset, you fail to consider the cost of inaction. You might think you exhibit such behavior only for minor consequences, but that isn't true. Take for example, vaccinations, which are essential to keep people healthy. Without them, you turn vulnerable to lethal diseases. Yet, some parents refuse to vaccinate their children due to the possible side effects. 3.3% of the US parents refused vaccination, fearing the consequences. While the vaccines can cause side effects in rare cases, the chances of falling victim to diseases by refusing vaccines are much higher. Yet, parents choose not to vaccinate their children to avoid an unlikely disaster. Even though inaction in this case can lead to death, it creates a fake moral comfort for the brain.

When you worry about your business failing, you decide to continue with your current job. That seems like a reasonable choice when you only consider the risk of failure. But, what about the pain involved with sticking to your current situation forever? Are you happy accepting the manager who looks down upon you all the time? Can you live a life of mediocrity for decades to come? Do you accept waking up every Monday and cursing the week ahead?

The consequences of your inaction often go unnoticed while you suffer in silence with regret. When you pause to make a choice, consider the price that you have to pay for not making any decision. Often, it could be higher.

The above examples might appear as if I am providing contradicting advice. You might complain, "You just said I must ask myself what the guarantee of success is when I quit my job. Now you are telling me to consider the cost of sticking to my current job. Which one should I follow?" Unfortunately, I cannot decide that for you. You know yourself and your situation better than anybody else does. The reason behind the contradicting advice is because I am not advocating any side. For some, quitting their job is a wise choice, while for others sticking to their profession is. The purpose of the 2-second principle is to help you decide by considering the pros and cons. It helps you look at both sides of the coin before making the call.

In the next chapter, we will talk about empathy. You think you understand others well, don't you? Think again. Most of us know the topic of empathy, but fail to apply it. In the upcoming chapter, you will learn to use the 2-second principle to develop compassion towards your partner, coworkers, friends, and the rest of the world.

Current Chapter in short

- How you make decisions on impulse
- The another choice syndrome
- The risk-loving and the risk-averse mindset
- How to take risks the right way
  - When you feel like taking a risk
    - Wait
    - Ask yourself if the reward is based on your assumption
    - Ask yourself what the guarantee is
  - When you feel risk-averse

- Ask yourself if you have considered the cost of inaction

CHAPTER 6

The huge rewards we give ourselves that we don't deserve

I observed a strange behavior in myself when I was writing one of the chapters for this book. What can be a better example than me being the culprit while writing this exact book?

I had set a daily target for the number of words I write to ensure I complete the book on time. The figure would vary based on the day of the week. The goal for that day was to write 3000 words. Since I am a blogger, some chapters of this book have content from previously written blog posts. But, I cannot simply copy and paste the whole article from my blog to the book. I have to rewrite them to fit the context and the flow. However, for the chapter I was writing that day, I could reuse a big chunk of the existing article with minimal edits. It took me less than a quarter of the time to complete 3000 words compared to what I usually needed.

So what did I do next? I patted myself on the back, relaxed on the couch, and turned on Netflix. I had given myself a reward I did not deserve. Could I have spent the time saved to actually "write" 3000 words? Yes. But I convinced myself that I had "written" 3000 words when I had copy-pasted most of them. No one was watching. No one was judging. No one was complaining. I was lying to myself to justify my actions and feel better in my own eyes. Such behavior manifests itself in big ways and small.

Let me take a typical example from a normal day at work. I have heard many other people complain about the same problem. Every day, I write the list of things to do for the day in a notebook and keep it next to me. Some tasks take hours to complete, while some take only minutes. Sometimes, soon after completing a small task, I feel I deserve a break. All I did was complete the task of sending a few pending emails which barely took 10 minutes. Yet, I feel like leaning back on my chair to relax. I open my phone to watch a Youtube video as a reward for the menial job. On some occasions, I have watched a few videos back to back, spending 15 minutes in total. I gave myself a reward of wasting 15 minutes for completing a task which took 10 minutes. Doesn't that seem stupid? Sure, it does. But when you analyze yourself closely, you will notice how often that happens.

Here are some examples where you lie to yourself:

- You believe you deserve a drink after a long working day
- You feel you have earned the right to buy yourself a lavish lunch because you saved some money
- You convince yourself you deserve a new watch because you got a bonus
- You tell yourself you need a new pair of clothes because you haven't shopped in months

The thought process behind lying to yourself

You are the best critic you will ever have. Whenever you perform some action, you make an unconscious judgment of whether your decision is good or bad. Before making a wrong decision, a court case takes place within you. The exciting part is, you fight against yourself. Two lawyers are fighting the case, and you are the judge making the final decision. The logical lawyer argues that you're doing the wrong thing. But the crooked lawyer within you brings in false evidence to convince the judge, aka you, about the action.

Take for example, the act of eating junk food after working out. You know that eating those bad calories nullifies the benefit that comes out of the workout, yet, you're craving for tasty food. Now your mind faces a dilemma, and it turns into a case to solve. The logical lawyer argues that eating junk is stupid. The crooked lawyer, however, justifies how you deserved it because you ran like a horse and lifted weights like a bodybuilder from Mr. Olympia. In reality, all you did was run for 15 minutes on the treadmill and lifted the lighter dumbbells. Yet, the deceitful lawyer exaggerates your actions. You bring in false evidence to convince yourself. The act of wrongdoing invokes a pang of guilt within you. The moment guilt comes into the picture, the crooked lawyer wants to find a reason to justify the action. If he can't identify a firm cause, he fabricates an excuse. The judge within you is the final decision-maker. Unfortunately, the judge, by nature, is naive and operates primarily on emotions. He makes decisions based on how strong the arguments were.

The judge makes rational decisions in two cases:

Past bad experience

If you had made a wrong decision before and suffered the consequences, you control your choices better. If you had eaten tons of calories in the past listening to the wrong lawyer and gained weight, you would have observed the result on the weighing scale. You might repeat the same wrong decision a few times, but sooner or later, you will realize the root cause. No matter how persuasive and authoritative the crooked lawyer is, sooner or later, you will know he is lying. After burning your fingers and learning the hard way, the judge within you will ignore the bad lawyer.

Self-training

If you want the judge within you to make decisions based on facts, you have to train him. The judge has to understand not to take the arguments of the lousy lawyer at face value. If not, he will persuade you almost always.

Now, do not assume that the judge knows how to recognize the crooked lawyer. A different lawyer shows up for each case. You do not know who the honest lawyer is and who is bringing in fake evidence. For example, after a few mistakes, you learn to identify the devious lawyer who convinces you to eat junk food. You know about the false arguments and bogus evidence he brings to the table. But, if you are deciding to buy an expensive watch, the same bad lawyer won't show up. Another corrupt lawyer will fight the case, who shows up in an Armani suit with a neatly trimmed beard and uses different tactics to persuade you. Though you ignored the bad lawyer of junk calories yesterday, this deceitful guy convinces you to spend money. You assume he was suggesting valid reasons to splurge the big bucks.

You have to train yourself to differentiate the honest lawyer from the other scoundrel. The most effective way to do so is to think of the consequences of your actions. You can determine the real face of the lawyer by using the 2-second principle. I will get to that at the end of the chapter.

The concept of moral licensing

The bad lawyer does not only justify wrongdoing but also sabotages the results from your excellent work. As per psychology, moral licensing is the process of fooling ourselves to justify shabby behavior using other good actions. Some call the tendency self-licensing. The phenomenon manifests in two ways:

1. Your past good actions warranting the current bad actions

After completing a positive action, you feel you have the license to do something bad. For example, if you did not drink alcohol for the last few days, you believe you can visit the bar today. You might also feel like ordering a few extra pegs of scotch because you controlled yourself all these days.

2. Your future plans justifying the current behavior

When you make a plan to stop a bad habit or cultivate a good habit, you believe you can over-indulge in poor behavior until you begin. For example, if you plan to start eating healthy next month, you provide yourself the privilege of binge eating till then. You find yourself worthy of a treat because you assume you will burn all the calories soon.

Several studies have shown how well known public figures have displayed behavior that contradicted what they preached. Research has also shown how people who express disagreement over sexist hiring have a higher chance of selecting a guy for a male-dominated job. Similarly, people who expressed their support for Obama as the President have displayed acts of racism in their lives. Once people have carried out deeds of virtue, they feel their unethical behavior is justified. By the way, people aren't lying to themselves intentionally. They genuinely believe they are doing the right thing.

Have you observed what happens to the people who win a lottery? Stories have shown how most people go back to their old state of financial affairs after a big win. The extra money in their account becomes a reason to go on a trip around the world, buy a lavish sports car, and replace the furniture in the house. The same logic applies to many people who earn money gambling. They cannot hold on to what they win because they consider it free money.

"I have never won a lottery, and I do not have the habit of gambling," you think. What do you do with the bonus you earn every year? Many believe that the extra bucks serve as money to spend on needless expenses. Logically speaking, once the bonus hits your account, it is no different from your salary because it is your money, and it's in your bank account. Yet, you view the additional figure as a standalone pile of extra cash that you have the license to spend. When you receive some money you did not expect, you find a reason to blow it all.

How to use the 2-second principle to avoid undeserved rewards

Again, you can use the ask a question technique during the pause to avoid giving yourself the rewards you do not deserve. Here are some of the questions you can ask:

Do I deserve it?

You tend to reward yourself in proportions greater than the effort put in. Ask yourself if you deserve the reward. When you want to take a 20-minute break after a 30-minute task, your inner conscience knows you are lazing around. All it takes is asking yourself. You cannot lie to yourself comfortably when you can ask a direct question because you will feel a pinch inside you saying, "Ok, that's enough, stop lying, you idiot. Whom are you trying to fool?"

Am I lying to myself?

Some of us have a natural skill at lying. I have a good friend who has a reason up his sleeve every time something goes wrong. The most common scenario is when he arrives late. Ask him why and he has a reason right off the bat like a magician pulling rabbits out of a hat.

"Had to send a last-minute email to a client who asked for a critical change."
"The road was closed due to a vehicle breaking down, and I had to take an alternate route."

What baffles me is, he doesn't come up with fake reasons beforehand. He makes them up on the spot. It is a natural skill ingrained within him. So, if you're such a person, you will find the previous question easy to justify. The liar within you will tell you, "Damn right, I deserve it." To avoid such excuses, you can instead ask yourself, "Am I lying to myself?" Now lying to the question which is asking if you're lying, isn't simple even for the habitual liars.

Am I damaging my efforts?

You can control the damage of moral licensing by asking yourself if you're hurting your own effort. It isn't hard to realize that junk food after working out nullifies all the hard work you put in. The hardest part is accepting the truth and doing the right thing. The bad lawyer within you screams out a million reasons why you should go the wrong way while the good lawyer sits in the corner and opposes with a feeble voice.

The Magic Of 2 Seconds

When you ask yourself if the action will damage the effort, the lousy lawyer's arguments seem weak. You feel guilty for wasting the time and energy you've already put in. Lying to yourself isn't easy at all. As human beings, we have found a sneaky way to avoid lying to ourselves, which is bypassing the question itself.

Have you noticed a known person walking in the opposite direction, increased your walking speed, and sped past him without making any eye contact on purpose? You did that because you wanted to pretend you did not notice him at all. Your brain does the same when you are about to perform a little act of wrongdoing. It pretends to avoid eye contact with the truth and rushes through with the action.

The 2-second principle puts a pause to such pretense. It's like the other person calling out your name and saying hi. Sure, you can act deaf too, but you wouldn't do that, would you? That seems way too obvious to sneak out of. Likewise, asking yourself a question makes it difficult to escape the truth you're already aware of. Your inner conscience is one of the most ethical decision-makers. The caveat is, the actions it suggests aren't always easy to perform. To avoid that discomfort, you muffle the voice of your conscience itself.

The 2-second principle forces you to stop and listen to the moral voice within you. When you start sweeping your mistakes under the rug, it holds a torchlight and says, "Look, there is your filth. Clean it up."

In the next chapter, we will look at our lazy side. We like to do as little as possible and procrastinate our tasks to the next day. You can use the 2-second principle to overcome some of your little acts of laziness.

Current Chapter in short

- How you reward yourself for little acts
- The reason why you lie to yourself to justify the reward
- How the lawyers within you fight to make a decision
- How you morally license your wrongdoing
- Using the ask a question technique to prevent undeserved rewards
    - Do I deserve it?
    - Am I lying to myself?
    - Am I damaging my efforts?

CHAPTER 7

The Lazy Demon inside you

No matter who you are, no matter what you do, you will exhibit laziness in some shape or form. Some of you will nod your head accepting your lethargy while the hard workers will draw their swords to challenge me. Let me explain. Laziness does not always show itself like a boulder. It occurs like little pebbles which are hard to notice.

If you had to draw laziness as a picture, what would you portray? Try to imagine what your sketch would look like. Do you have an image in your head?

Did you visualize a person lying on the couch and eating junk food? Or did you imagine someone sleeping? In any case, people associate laziness with lack of physical activity. You tend to call a person lazy if he prefers to stay on the couch, refuses to workout, or fails to complete basic tasks. But laziness shows up in different forms, many of which are much smaller to notice.

Let me tell you one such case of my laziness which appears minuscule. I have a love for books and I spend at least an hour every day reading. When I'm reading, I encounter powerful topics, exciting thoughts, and interesting ideas that can make a great blog post. All I need to do is pull the phone out of my pocket and make a note. Yet, what do I do? I tell myself, "You have a great memory. You do not need to write it down." If we had statistics on lies, that one would bag the second place. Certainly, the first place goes to the well known "I am on my way."

I have forgotten my thought and regretted not having writing an idea down a bazillion times. Yet, I still feel lazy and repeat the mistake. Soon after, I wrack my brain trying to recall the thought until the nerves on my head pop out, but I come up with nothing. These simple forms of laziness go unnoticed. Most people do not even consider such misses as laziness.

There are three primary areas where we exhibit laziness.

1. Trivial Tasks
2. Intermediate tasks
3. Major projects

Trivial Tasks

These are simple tasks like writing a thought down, which barely require any extra energy or effort. Other examples include:

- Replying to an email right now which requires a one-liner response instead of leaving it for later
- Returning a missed call instead of planning to do it in the evening
- Leaving the empty can of soda on the couch instead of dropping it in the trash
- Throwing the keys at a random place instead of placing them on the keyholder

The reason why you procrastinate such tasks is that you know you can complete them later with ease. But, the tricky part is, what is easy to do is also easy to not do. When Newton said, "Objects in motion stay in motion while objects at rest stay at rest", little did he know that his law applied to human beings too.

Intermediate tasks

These tasks require more effort than simply pulling out your phone or typing an email. Some examples include:

- Organizing your cupboard instead of stuffing things everywhere(A big culprit myself)
- Cooking food instead of ordering dinner
- Doing your laundry every week instead of waiting to run out of clean clothes

The reason why you procrastinate such tasks is because of the effort involved. You prefer instant gratification instead of spending energy because the consequences are not that severe. Postponing these tasks does not affect you with a single instance. But such procrastination happens so often that it turns into a habit that harms you in the long term.

Major Projects

These are tasks that require a humongous effort to pull off and also come with huge returns. You cannot finish them in a day or two. You need months or years to accomplish them. Some examples include:

- Pursuing your long term goal
- Losing 25 pounds
- Improving a vital life skill such as communication

The reason why you procrastinate such tasks is:

- Taking the first step seems hard
- The results seem too far or uncertain
- The effort involved seems overwhelming

Procrastinating major projects leads to long term regret and a life of mediocrity. You sacrifice a better possible future return in exchange for a smaller but guaranteed current reward. Tim Urban explains how the mind of a procrastinator works. Each one of us has a rational decision-maker and an instant gratification monkey within our brain. One wants you to get work done, while the other urges you to waste time.

Every time you have to perform a task, the monkey reminds you to browse social media, watch Netflix, or read the newspaper. Let's say you have to complete a massive project which will need over three months of effort. Though you know the amount of work involved, you let the first month pass by because you listen to the monkey. In the second month, you feel more regret and stress about not starting any work. Nevertheless, you still do not begin. When it comes down to the last month, you find yourself sweating, anxious, and worried. This is the point where the panic monster enters the picture. You scuffle to finish the pending work in a hurry when the monster shows up because he is the only thing the instant gratification monkey is scared of. With distractions out of the picture and reality sinking in, you slog late hours and weekends to pull off the project.

You might think that the panic monster is the savior of all procrastinators, but he does not show up every single time. Two important criteria trigger him to appear:

- Consequences - He shows up only when the consequences are severe, like losing your job, getting bad scores, facing public embarrassment, and so on.
- Deadline - He makes an appearance when the time to complete the task approaches closer. Until you're running short of time, you will not spot him anywhere and continue listening to the monkey.

If the outcome causes minimal damage that you can deal with, like failing to clean the cupboard, the panic monster remains in deep slumber. You brush off the consequences and move on. But the area where you miss the panic monster the most is your long term goals. For example, if you want to start your business venture, there are neither stipulated deadlines nor significant consequences. Sure, you can set some timelines for yourself, but you have the privilege to push them further at your sole discretion. Also, even if you do not start a business, you will sail through life with a regular job.

Without the fear of consequences or deadlines, you have no reason to panic. Without panic, there is no panic monster. Without the panic monster, your dream remains a dream. Regret turns into a daily affair, and your daily routine turns into a grind for life.

The main reason for laziness

Why do you think you choose to be lazy instead of putting effort? Take any example:

- Tossing the phone aside with a mental note to reply to the text message later
- Postponing studies till the fag end of the exam
- Hitting the snooze button
- Procrastinating working out hoping to start next Monday
- Pushing the first action towards your long term goal to the next month
- Watching another Netflix episode instead of cleaning your cupboard

Did you notice that the above tasks are diverse in nature? Some are menial tasks, while others require enormous time and energy. Each of them also comes with a reward proportional to the effort required. Irrespective of the magnitude of the reward, they all have something in common. Can you spot it? The common area is - the reward for each task comes at the cost of your present comfort. This is how all the mentioned tasks disrupt your convenience:

- You have to put some thought and effort into replying to the text
- You have to get your butt off the couch and start studying now to score good grades
- You have to sacrifice your sleep to wake up
- You have to sweat it out today to lose weight
- You have to make time to start working on your long term goal
- You have to sacrifice the pleasure of a Netflix episode and get work done

We all live in the present, and the current comfort comes with a natural temptation. We tend to prefer instant gratification over a long term reward. A low hanging fruit seems like a better option right now than a fruit basket in the future. Human beings are wired to spend as little energy as possible by default. From evolution, expending minimal energy makes sense because it helped us survive. The workouts or the marathons are not a part of evolution. By instinct, your brain will prevent you from spending energy. When choosing between two tasks, none of which you are passionate about, your mind picks the one that requires lesser effort.

How to avoid laziness?

You can avoid procrastinating using the 2-second rule.

The Magic Of 2 Seconds

The lazy demon in your head keeps saying, "Postpone the task. Enjoy right now and take care of it later." When you feel the urge to postpone, pause for a moment. Use the technique of asking yourself questions like.

1. Is it easier to do it right now?

When you postpone a task for later, you will need more effort and energy to complete it. To prevent procrastinating, you can follow the 2 Minute Rule from David Allen's book "Getting things done." The rule states, "If a task takes less than 2 minutes to complete, you must do it right now even if it isn't important."

If you are heading for a break but notice an email that requires a quick reply, do it right away. If you see your to-do list and notice a quick pending call, pick the phone and dial the number. The rule commands never postponing any task which requires less than 2 minutes to complete. Completing the task later takes longer. Try adding up the time needed to remember the task, the information associated, and finally doing it. You will need more than 2 minutes later, so finish it off then and there.

2. What are the consequences if I miss it altogether?

You procrastinate a task for later without thinking enough. If you use the pause to ask yourself the consequences of forgetting a trivial task completely, you will feel the pinch. If you are about to decide to reply to an email later, ask yourself what if it slips off your mind altogether? The same applies to long term projects too. Visualize what could happen if you score bad grades by not studying. You would lose the subject, need an extra year to complete your studies, hamper your career growth, and so on. When you look at a task, you look at it as a job to do than the outcomes it can lead to. Use your pause to tweak that perspective. Consider what your procrastination can cause, and it will prompt you to act right away.

3. What are the benefits of doing it now?

The previous question uses fear to drive action. You can switch your thought process by framing the question in an alternative way. Looking for benefits is just another version of "What are the consequences of missing the action?" Some people are motivated by positive reinforcement than the fear of consequences. If you had to start working out, what would help you pick up your running shoes? The worry of a cardiac arrest or the joy of having a hot body? The cardiac arrest induces action due to fear of consequences. The thought of a toned body and the pleasure associated with attracting more members of the opposite sex drives action due to the benefits. You will find it hard to pin down one approach which works best for you. This is because your motivation can change based on different reasons:

Your personality and approach to life: Let us take an example of a choice you have to make - whether you should light the cigarette in your hand or not. One person finds better motivation because he is challenging himself to fight the urge. Another person finds motivation due to a longer life span.

The action behind the decision: If you are aiming to stop smoking, fear works as a better motivator. Most people quit smoking due to the fear of chronic diseases in the future rather than the benefit of better respiration and a longer life span. But, if you want to save money, the comfort of a large amount of wealth can induce better action. Here, the benefit serves as the motivation to take action. Depending on the task at hand, what motivates you can vary.

The Magic Of 2 Seconds

Your mental and emotional state while making the decision:
If a person close to you was diagnosed with a chronic ailment due to smoking, the fear can impact your actions. Though you always knew about the risks involved, specific events can serve as a compelling trigger to take action. As you start asking yourself a question during the pause, you will learn which one suits you best.

Does that seem like too many ifs and buts for 2 seconds? Don't worry. Your brain will make this process unconscious and lightning fast with a little practice. Avoiding tiny acts of laziness changes your life in ways you cannot fathom. If you watch yourself from an overhead camera, you will notice how often you procrastinate these small activities. Trying to fix prominent forms of procrastination like working towards your dreams isn't always easy. You tend to worry more about postponing your long term goals alone while those little acts of laziness slip right under your nose. Because the impact of completing(or not completing) the smaller tasks seem insignificant, you ignore them. But these are the little areas which compound together to make a difference to your dreams.

A small chunk of snow looks insignificant and tiny. But when it adds up, it can send a giant snowball down a mountain. Likewise, avoiding those little acts of laziness seems barely useful. Add them all together, and they make you as powerful as a boulder surging forward with momentum towards your dreams, destroying any obstacle on the path.

Using the power of the 2-second principle, you can battle your laziness. Depending on how lazy you are and how willing you are to listen to yourself, your results will vary. But you will make better decisions to overcome laziness if you pause to make a conscious choice. If you are lazy to apply the 2-second principle itself, I am afraid I do not have any other solution for you. Sure, you may forget to pause when you start trying the technique, but you'll get the hang of it with repetition.

In the next chapter, we will analyze your thought process. Human beings tend to believe that their style of doing things is the best way. Not only does this apply to actions but also to beliefs. You can apply the 2-second principle to avoid such arrogance and narrow-minded thinking.

Current Chapter in short

- Three primary areas where we exhibit laziness
- The main reason for laziness
- How to avoid laziness by asking yourself questions
  - Is it easier to do it right now?
  - What are the consequences if I miss it altogether?
  - What are the benefits of doing it now?

References:

Urban, Tim. (2013). Why Procrastinators Procrastinate? Wait But Why. https://waitbutwhy.com/2013/10/why-procrastinators-procrastinate.html

CHAPTER 8

My way or the highway

I had the habit of thinking that my style of doing things was the best. In recent years, I have realized how two people can have polar opposite opinions and still be right in their own way. When someone else had a different style or a contradicting view, I felt the need to prove myself right with facts and figures.

For example, I am an outright non-vegetarian. Back in the days, I would consider vegetarians foolish for staying away from delicious food. I have ridiculed countless people by asking them how can they survive on shoots and leaves. I have also noticed other people behave just like I did. The meat lovers would argue about the importance of proteins. Our rival group would explain how a vegan diet serves the body better. Nobody would change their belief though. The only outcome would be a needless debate that went nowhere.

Over time I have realized the stupidity of trying to push my own beliefs as right. When I started looking at others' opinions with an open mind without trying to find fault, I started realizing my mistakes. I now understand the importance of different perspectives. I knew about the importance of empathy for a long time, but applying it was a different ball game altogether. Understanding the viewpoint of others is no easy feat. On paper, empathy seems like a simple concept of understanding what the other person is feeling. In real life, when the other person disagrees with you, your brain prefers a debate or a fight instead of applying empathy.

As human beings, no one likes to lose or be proven wrong. Such behavior is acceptable in a contest or a sporting event. But you might not realize how such a mindset also seeps into your day to day life. When someone brings up a fact or an argument against your belief, you jump into challenging the person with a counter-argument. Winning provides a dopamine rush, which is a pleasure chemical that makes you feel better. Therefore, you try to win every debate possible solely for the sake of winning.

Take for example, a couple fighting over little issues. Most couples quarrel like two young siblings fighting for the last candy. The kids learn to behave with age, but a husband and wife don't. I wish someone could gather the statistics behind why people fight. I believe data would reveal that most issues arise because people fail to understand the other side.

Most fights occur because partners assume being in love implies both people should have the same point of view on every topic. Women consider spending on makeup as a necessity while men splurge on watching a sports event live. When the husband does not talk much, the wife assumes he has an extramarital affair when all he had was a stressful week. When the wife texts and smiles, the husband thinks she is getting cozy with a male colleague while all she was doing was gossiping with her lady friend. If all couples in the world realized that neither will women think like men nor will men behave like women, the earth would turn into a happier place within a snap of fingers.

Such differences do not occur between couples alone. Let's shift the topic from understanding personal relationships to disagreements at the workplace. Every organization has different kinds of people. The higher the number of employees, the more contrasting the personalities are. People who think alike tend to form a group even if they do not consciously create one. Here are some examples:

- Men and women
- The freshers and the experienced
- The people who leave on time and those who stay back late
- The experimenters and the by the book employees
- The party lovers and the sober folks

These segregations are examples and they will differ in your organization. If an organization's culture welcomes and encourages a mixed bag of people, ideas flow, and results flourish. But if one group starts contradicting the approach of another, things turn toxic. More often than not, that's what happens.

The experimenters wonder why can't everyone think of creative ideas as they do. The employees who go by the book cannot fathom how big companies can run without detailed documents and processes. Those who work long hours look at people who leave on time as laid back. The people who work by the clock assume the people who stay late have no life. Different people have different styles to suit different needs. It is incorrect to consider your style as the perfect way of doing things. One of the primary roles for leaders in such organizations is to foster a culture where people can work as a team amidst their differences.

Other examples of failing to apply empathy

Offensive sarcasm

When you make a sarcastic comment to crack a joke, your words can hurt people. On one occasion, we were in a group talking about random topics. One member of the group started bragging about his workout routines. Apparently, he had begun working out to lose weight in the last 2 weeks. He went on and on about his stamina, the variety of his exercises, fitness levels, and so on. After a point, I got fed up with the hot air he was blowing in the room. In the heat of the moment, I snapped, "So where is your six-pack?" The guy was overweight and had self-esteem issues for a long time. My sarcastic joke hit him hard. His excitement turned into agony before I had even completed the sentence. I realized my blunder within seconds and also apologized immediately, but the damage was done.

A comment can seem like a sarcastic joke on a lighter note when it forms in your head. The moment you spit it out, it can take a different turn altogether. A poorly worded joke can create more conflict than an offensive remark.

Thinking of a reply while the other person is talking

Read through the sentences below. These sentences are universally correct about every person. "You always consider your ideas better than that of others. Whenever someone presents their idea, you counter them for no reason. Even if your best friend gives you some advice, you will not agree right away."

By the way, I lied. Those words aren't valid for every person. But did you find yourself thinking of a reply as you read each of the 3 sentences? Most people do. Try to analyze yourself when you hold a conversation. Your brain tends to think of a reply for each sentence the other person says. As you prepare a response, you fail to concentrate on the words and the message the other person wants to convey. You will hear what the other person said, but you won't listen. When you prepare a solid reply in your head, your brain ignores the next few sentences the other person said.

Do you find yourself often asking the question, "Sorry, I did not catch what you said. What was that again?" If yes, you do not listen attentively enough. The right approach to a conversation is to hear the person out, process the words, emotions, and body language. Only after the other person finishes his words should you think of a response. Listening to understand differs significantly from merely hearing the words.

Turning down ideas

When someone asks you for feedback, how do you respond? Have you observed how you hunt for negative feedback first before finding positive elements? Let me tell you about my recent experience with the negative feedback instinct.

A friend of mine approached me with a question. "I am looking for your advice on my business idea." I agreed, and he went on with his thought. I pondered for a bit and told him the following. "The market you are targeting seems quite small. Also, the idea involves many complicated elements making it a toughie to execute. To make it worse, you will have a hard time scaling up."

If you break down all the feedback I had given, you will notice that I had only given negative feedback. In hindsight, I found many aspects of the idea brilliant. But what did my mind focus on? It found all the reasons why things could go wrong. The positives took a backseat and never occurred to me. The negative feedback instinct is your tendency to spot flaws first. Even if there are good things to talk about, the negatives come to your mind in an instant. You may find some positives to talk about or none at all.

Let us go through some examples:

1. A coworker asks you what you think about the email she is about to send. You either find a better flow for the email or suggest an alternative word to use. If not anything, you find an error in grammar or punctuation.

2. Your friend asks your opinion on the theme of her wedding. Your first reaction usually is: "Isn't that too dull for an outdoor event?" or "That's quite common these days. How about ..."

In both these examples, you feel like suggesting an improvement.

Consider the next two examples:

3. Your friend constructed a new house. He invites you home for dinner. When he is pouring a glass of wine, he asks you, "What do you think of the house?" You reply saying, "It looks fantastic and neatly done." However, in the back of your head, you tell yourself, "If this were my house, I would place the couch on the other side."

4. You are at a wedding, and your cousin asks you, "How is my dress?" You reply, "You look so pretty." But in silence, you wonder, "Wouldn't a darker color suit her and the occasion better?"

In the last two examples, you do not mention an improvement, but your mind finds one flaw or the other. Such behavior applies to every single person. If you are a leader of a group, you need to be even more conscious of this instinct. If you turn down ideas or find flaws with every suggestion, people will stop approaching you. You build a reputation of a jerk who knows nothing better than finding faults every time.

How failing to understand the perspective of others affects you

On the surface, the need to understand other people seems unimportant. You might even shrug it off, thinking it hardly makes any difference. But, it makes a ton of a difference. Being empathetic about the feelings, beliefs, and opinions of others helps you look at the world in a whole new light. The difference is as significant as watching the TV in Blu-Ray vs. The usual resolution. The context is the same, but you can view the picture with a lot more detail. Here is what happens when you fail to look at things from a different perspective:

Loss of opportunity to learn

Bring any two people in a room, and both will have something to learn from each other, guaranteed. Yes, any two people. One could be Elon Musk, while the other could be a person whom the society considers a failure. Yet, each person will know about some topic which the other doesn't. Every conversation you have provides you an opportunity to improve yourself. If you have the humility to examine the perspective of the other person with an open mind, you can tap into the benefits of different viewpoints. You do not have to agree with the other person, but at least you can make an effort to understand where the other person is coming from

Less co-operation

If you turn down an opinion, the other person will brush off your action the first time. Do it again, and the person will sense a tinge of resentment. Repeat the same enough number of times, and you will come across as a person who has the habit of contradicting opinions. Over time, people stop cooperating with you because human beings reciprocate what they receive. Maybe, not everyone will do so. Neither will such behavior always be intentional. But the world around you will look at you as someone they are not very keen to help.

Hiding their opinion

When you build a routine of challenging others' thoughts, people stop expressing their viewpoint due to the fear of a backlash. They keep their opinions to themselves which otherwise would have added valuable input to the conversation. The behavior can have drastic consequences if a person in authority often proves other people wrong unintentionally. Such actions have caused many tragedies, for example, the Avianca 52 Flight disaster killed 73 passengers.

The Avianca disaster happened because the ATC failed to understand that the copilot was explaining the dire situation of the flight. The copilot was at fault too, because he was unable to explain the urgency of the situation. But when the ATC turned down the request for an emergency landing, the pilot was hesitant to convey the importance of landing immediately. The event forever changed the model of communication between the pilots and the ATC staff.

When people share their opinion, and you shoot it down, they do not express their thoughts comfortably the next time.

An exercise to find out how much you contradict

You might assume you do not contradict the opinion of others. To find how often you do, try this exercise. On any given day, count the number of sentences you start with the words – no, but, however. When you use these words to begin a sentence, it indicates you disagree with the other person one way or another. You can use all the diplomatic words to sugar coat your message, but you are still opposing the other person's belief. When I tried the exercise the first time, I was shell shocked to reach a total of over 35 by 4 PM. At that point, I stopped counting for the day. What stumped me was, I always considered myself an approachable person. I have improved since then, and my tally now comes to single digits a day, but I slip into the behavior of contradicting people quite often. The exercise of counting "no, but, however", was a part of the book What Got You Here Won't Get You There by Marshall Goldsmith.

Make no mistake, you do not have to agree with every single opinion thrown at you and turn into a people pleaser. But, try to make a conscious effort to understand what the other person is saying before agreeing or disagreeing. You will build better relationships, get into fewer arguments, develop greater rapport, and facilitate smoother communication. But knowing whether you should challenge an opinion, change your belief or agree to disagree is an art that comes with experience and practice. I am far from achieving it and working towards getting better at it.

How to apply the 2-second principle for better empathy

For me, empathy is the area where the 2-second principle helps the most. I have heard many other people admitting that failing to apply empathy is the most common mistake they make on impulse. Use the pause to ask yourself a few questions. In a second, you can transform your thinking from self-centered and narrow-minded to compassionate and empathetic. Here are some questions you can ask yourself:

Do I need to say or do this right now?

Your mind thinks of a reply to fill the silence, make conversation, crack a joke, or refute an argument. Though you might have a valid point to make, saying what you have in mind right away isn't always the best move. I have demotivated many people by turning down ideas and explaining why they won't work. In most cases, I was honest, and my feedback was valid. The problem was, I went straight into decline mode.

Today, I use a different approach. If anyone comes to me with an idea, I do not refute it right away. I either ask for time to think or bring up my thoughts during the next conversation. Introduce a gap between the time the idea was presented and the time you deliver the feedback. If you do, you increase the chances of the other person welcoming your feedback. Likewise, use the pause to ask yourself if you need to say or do what you have in mind right away. Many a time, you can postpone your actions and achieve more acceptance. Procrastination isn't always bad.

Do my words/actions make things better?

Whatever you say or do induces a reaction, good or bad. If your words or actions lead to better outcomes, they make sense. If not, what purpose do they serve? Ask yourself if your remark or actions make things better in one of the following ways:

- Help the person correct himself or bring about a change
- Make the person feel better for the right reasons(not fake buttering)

A common mistake people make is passing a comment about an error that can no longer be rectified. One day when my wife left the electric grill on, the chicken got toasted black. "You should have turned it off on time," I told her. In hindsight, I realized I was Captain Obvious. Yes, everyone knows that leaving the switch on for longer than necessary burns the food. What good was my comment? Providing a suggestion to set a reminder next time would have been far more useful. If your words or actions do not help anyone, you are better off keeping them to yourself. If an event can neither be changed nor prevented from occurring again, you rather not talk about it.

Can I say or do this at a better time?

This question is an alternate version of the first question. Reversing the question can force your mind to think the other way. When you ask yourself if you need to say something now, you start hunting for a yes or no answer. When you ask yourself if you can find a better time to say the same thing, your brain starts looking for a more suitable occasion. Same question, but different answers.

Practicing empathy in real life is much harder than talking about it. You need conscious effort and mindfulness to understand how another person is feeling.

In the next chapter, we will go through examples of why partners have difficulty understanding each other. You will also apply the 2-second principle to care for and understand your partner and develop a stronger relationship.

Current chapter in short

- You tend to stick to your style and way of thinking
- Examples of how you fail to apply empathy
- Offensive sarcasm
- Thinking of a reply instead of listening
- Turning down ideas

- How failing to understand the perspective of others affects you
- An exercise to find out how much you contradict
- How to apply the 2-second principle for better empathy by asking yourself:
  - Do I need to say or do this right now?
  - Do my words/actions make things better?
  - Can I say or do this at a better time?

References:

Goldsmith, Marshall, and Mark Reiter. "The Twenty Habits." In What Got You Here Won't Get You There: How Successful People Become Even More Successful. London: Profile Books, 2013.

CHAPTER 9

I can't understand why my partner does that

After I got married and moved in with my wife, I had a hard time digesting the change. As a bachelor, I would throw my wallet on the refrigerator, my shoes under the couch, and my socks next to the bed. If I felt lazy some weekend, I would spend the time by myself for the introvert I was. But once I was living with my wife, I could no longer enjoy some comfort that I had earlier taken for granted. Agreed that my habits weren't the best practices for a bachelor, but the change was uncomfortable. Have you watched a movie where the hero forgets the past and is taken aback about things around him? That's exactly how both of us felt. I am sure she had a hard time with the change herself.

Whether you are married or in a relationship, you will run into disagreements with your partner. The problems arise because you expect your partner to think, behave, and act as you do. To make that worse, your partner feels exactly the same from her perspective. Once you respect the thought process of your partner, all the disagreements vanish. That's how we reached a compromise. We still fight once in a while to remind ourselves that we are husband and wife, But overall, our arguments have drastically reduced. We disagree with each other, but we no longer see a need to agree for every little thing.

How little actions and words hurt relationships

In a relationship, sometimes you say things you should never have said and do things that you should never have done. I am not even referring to major screw-ups. I am only talking about little things that happen on impulse. Here are some examples:

1. Sarcastic comments

When you want to taunt your partner about something which annoyed you, you resort to sarcasm. Some of the sarcastic comments cross the line and turn into a real burn. When the wife says, "we should reduce eating outside," the husband replies, "We could do that if you learned how to cook better." When the husband says, "I am thinking of buying a second-hand car," the wife replies, "Had you found a better job, you could afford a brand new one." When the husband says, "I have put on belly fat recently," the wife says, "After hanging around with your friends and going out drinking often, were you expecting rock hard abs?" What was supposed to be a joke turns into a hurtful remark.

2. Starting with a taunt

Sometimes when you run out of patience, you complain about your partner for no reason as a defense mechanism. When your partner tells you that you threw your socks under the couch, you complain about the hair in the sink. A wise man has once said, an eye for an eye makes the world blind. But in a relationship, a comment for a comment makes both of them lose their mind. You can avoid many such quarrels using the 2-second principle. A word of caution though. No law or tip, including the 2-second principle, is capable of stopping all fights between a husband and wife. If someone knows one, my contact details are at the end of the book. Do reach out to me.

How to use the 2-second principle to make your day more productive

The Magic Of 2 Seconds

You can use both the wait and ask a question technique to avoid fights with your partner.

Waiting technique

In scenarios like these, the waiting technique is highly effective. When you feel things intensifying, and the situation heating up, pause and wait. All it takes is one second from one of the two people involved to not take the fight further. That's about it. Silence calms down more fights than rational arguments ever can.

When you're fighting with your partner, logic goes out the window before the quarrel even begins. The debate turns purely emotional, and both of you hunt back into memory to recall who erred, when they did make a mistake and why. It's like saving the best wine for the right occasion. Waiting it out is the best way to diffuse the emotion and the fight.

Ask a question technique

If you have the patience to ask yourself a question during a quarrel, that can work wonders too. You can ask yourself:

1. Will my words or action hurt my partner?

If you take a moment to analyze your sarcastic comment, you will know whether it can hurt your partner. You can avoid statements that sound reasonable in your head but come across as hurtful when you say them. Two words to be wary about are "never" and "always." When you use them to complain about your partner, you increase the chances of a fight. If a woman tells a man, "You never pay attention," it ends with an argument. If the man tells the woman, "You always take an hour to get ready," the lady will take an extra 10 minutes the next time to seek revenge. A better way of dealing with such issues is to talk about the change you're expecting.

"I would feel more valued if you paid more attention," will bring out a better response than a complaint with the word "never". "I would appreciate if you get ready sooner so that I have to wait lesser," will increase the chances of your wife listening. Use the pause to ask yourself if you're providing feedback the right way. A few corrected words and a couple of rephrased sentences is all it takes. You can trigger a fight or cause a change in behavior based on the words you use.

2. Is there a point in winning the argument?

Arguing with a friend or an unknown person has a different impact compared to how it affects your partner. A vow of silence for a few days or a tit for tat behavior hurts both people in the relationship. Before you argue or make a sharp remark which comes across as offensive, ask yourself if you need to win the argument. What is the point of having a more robust argument when both of you end up going to bed angry? The best result for some fights is to avoid it in the first place. The 2-second principle can help you do that.

3. Is my inaction hurting my partner?

An incorrect action isn't the only way of hurting your partner. Your inaction can have a worse effect. When the wife asks the husband to fix the leaking tap in the bathroom, it is not about the faucet alone. If the problem remains unaddressed for long, the husband's negligence annoys the wife more than the spilling water.

When the husband asks the wife to stop organizing to the point that nothing is easy to find, not making a change gets on his nerves. When your partner asks you to make a change, use the pause to ask yourself what the consequences of your inaction are. Sometimes, you have no intention to make a change, but you nod anyway. You assume your partner will forget it over time. Such inaction works against you because it gives the impression that you do not care about what your partner said. If you do not agree with the feedback or do not want to make a change, use the pause to remind yourself that you need to speak up. A disagreement in silence is sometimes more harmful than an argument over a conversation.

4. Ask if you're bringing in an unrelated problem into the discussion

A common practice between couples is to bring in an unrelated prior problem into an argument. When the wife says, "When will you start working out?," the husband replies, "You don't listen to me when I ask you to reduce shopping, do you?" When the husband says, "We'll have to visit a friend of mine this weekend," the wife says, "If spending long hours in office was not enough already, you started with the weekends too."

Strengthening your argument using an unrelated problem leads to a complaining session. Unless you want to listen to all your flaws, keep the talk to one problem at a time. Discussing multiple issues in one conversation turns into a more significant concern in itself. Before you make a counter-argument, pause and ask yourself, "Am I bringing an unnecessary concern into the limelight?" If you do, you will get one back yourself. You reap what you sow.

5. Ask yourself, "Am I listening or counter arguing"?

A disagreement between a couple can soon escalate into a problem listing competition. It is like an outlet for a dam. When it opens, water only splurges out, nothing gets in.

Likewise, in an argument, you worry only about what you have to say, without listening to a word. Use the pause to check on yourself if you're even listening.

Relationships don't grow stronger by themselves over time. It's like a sapling that has just sprouted. If you choose to nourish it with water, sunlight, and the right soil, the plant will bloom. While it is growing, a small slip can hurt it badly. If you completely neglect it, the plant will lose strength and die. Likewise, a relationship takes effort to flourish and a silly mistake can create a serious dent. The 2-second principle makes you more mindful about the little aspects of your relationship.

In the next chapter, we will go through our daily bad habits which impact our productivity. Millions of dreams go unrealized because people fail to perform the action required to pursue their goals. You will learn how to apply the 2-second principle to improve your productivity in little ways.

Current Chapter in short

- How little actions and words hurt relationships
- Sarcastic comments
- Starting with a taunt
- How to use the 2-second rule for better relationships
- Wait it out to diffuse the emotions
- Ask a question technique
  - Will my words or action hurt my partner?
  - Is there a point in winning the argument?
  - Is my inaction hurting my partner?
  - Ask if you're bringing in an unrelated problem into the discussion
  - Ask yourself am I listening or counter arguing?

CHAPTER 10

I did nothing useful today

Here is my story of how I used to go about my day earlier. After many mistakes, unproductive days, and years of experimentation, I figured a better approach. Let us rewind the clock 5 years back. "I will knock off all the important tasks on my to-do list," I told myself in the morning, rolling my sleeves in front of the dressing mirror. "I will ensure today is unlike other days," I said, determined to start the week on a positive note. Soon after I reached my workplace, I opened my emails. I saw one which wasn't exactly urgent, but I decided to work on it.

After spending some time on such emails and replying to others, an hour had already passed. Besides, I had picked up a few more things to work on, which had come up after I entered the office. By evening, all the plans I made in front of the mirror had gone down the drain. I had managed to work only on one or two essential tasks that mattered to me. My entire day had passed, attending to duties that were a priority to others. "Why can't I focus on the tasks which add value to my long term goals?" I murmured to myself as I rolled into bed, tucking the quilt over me.

The normal flow of events of an unproductive day

The morning begins with a mental plan to make the day as fruitful as possible. Once the day starts, you focus your attention on other tasks that seem important at the moment. One thing leads to another, and you lose sight of your long term goals because you cannot take your mind off these so-called "urgent tasks." More often than not, these tasks are not urgent. It is only your perception which convinces you to believe so. Here are a few examples where you spend time on a task you could have postponed:

- Answering every phone call as soon as your phone rings
- Working on an email as soon as you notice the notification
- Accepting a last-minute meeting

Think again. Do you need to react to such scenarios as you did? If you leave your phone on silent in the drawer, you won't realize that someone called. If the call was urgent, you could have returned the call after a while. Did people expect your email reply within 5 minutes? Or have you made a habit of replying to emails so fast that it has now become an expectation? Did you consider if the 30 minutes spent on the meeting would add any value? What if you chose to decline the meeting instead?

Based on what you do in life, the tasks in your bucket will vary. But no matter what your profession is, you spend unnecessary time on tasks that do not need immediate attention.

The most common productivity mistakes you make

1. Approaching the day as it comes

If you go by your day finishing one task after another based on what you feel, you are not making the best use of your time. Instead, you must have a plan to approach your day. No, you do not need a step by step roadmap like the one which puts a rocket into space. You don't need to schedule every 10 minutes of your day as some executives do either. What you need is a clear idea of the top 5 things you must accomplish on a given day. Most of them should align with your long term goals. If you have a to-do list, you assume you have a track on the things you need to work on.

Wrong!

I had a to-do list. Even after having a to-do list, I would end my day with a feeling that I could've done better. I was terrible at prioritizing and picking the right task to work. To-do lists grow longer over time, making it difficult to decide which task you should work on next. To make sure you work on the right tasks each day, spend 5-10 min to determine the most important things you need to complete that day. Writing those tasks on a notepad makes the plan even more robust and yields maximum productivity. Having a clear idea on your target for the day leads to a more productive day than going by a long to-do list.

2. Picking the easiest task to work on

When you have a long pending to-do list, you feel like knocking off the easiest one first. That's one item off the list, and you feel relieved about getting some work done. But such a mindset leads to poor prioritization. You must cultivate an approach of doing what is necessary than completing what is most comfortable. In the past, whenever I finished a task, I would scan through my to-do list to spot the next easiest one. Sometimes, I would go through the list twice to make sure nothing else was simpler. I would complete the task and then lean back on my chair and have a cup of coffee. I would end the day with many cups of coffee, a ton of breaks, a bunch of easy tasks completed, and a pile of incomplete important tasks.

Picking an easy task to work on is one form of procrastination. Completing a task feels like enough reason to deserve a break.

So one leads to another where you finally end up with all the vital work pending. "I did not have enough time today. So I will continue from here tomorrow," you tell yourself to feel better about how you spent your day. But really? Did you lack time to complete the important tasks? Of course not. You had enough and more. You chose to spend it in stupid ways.

3. Saying yes to everything

I had the habit of agreeing to anything that came my way. It was like I was carrying a board that said, "Ask me for anything. I will say yes."

If an email landed in my inbox, I would open it and reply right away. If a coworker sent me a meeting invite, I would accept without even checking what it was for. If someone had a task for me, I would work on it even if it added no value. I said yes to things like Jesus welcomed sinners with open arms.

The emails which land in your inbox can wait. Half the meetings you attend are a waste of time. Many of the tasks you work on add no value to your long term goals. Make a conscious effort to work on things that matter. Answer emails when time permits. Decline some meetings. If required, add a small note mentioning why you did so. You might even have to phrase your words with diplomacy to avoid bad sentiments. Do not work on tasks that you believe add no value. What you spend your time on must make a difference. If you do things without thinking enough, you are no different than the pig wiggling in the mud. Oh, wait, there is a difference. At least the pig is enjoying it.

How to use the 2-second principle to make your day more productive

The Magic Of 2 Seconds

You can use both the waiting and asking a question technique to make your day more efficient.

1. Wait

Many of the things you do work on throughout your day are impulsive reactions. When you see an email notification on the right top of your screen, you stop what you're doing and pounce on it. When you hear the buzz of the chat message you received on the instant messenger, you open it and reply instantly. Just wait for a moment and the urge will pass. Many of the emails and chats you receive do not need your attention. If they do, it is only because you have created an expectation of quick replies and only you can change that. A better solution to your problem is to mute notifications altogether and check them every few hours.

2. Ask yourself if the task adds value

Question every task you lay your hands on. If you receive a meeting invite, do not accept it unless you believe it drives action or provides useful information. If you have an item on your to-do list, ask yourself if completing the task adds any value. Too often, we end up doing tasks because someone asked us to or to knock them off the list. Always think if you can do something more valuable instead.

3. Ask yourself if you need to do the task right now

Sometimes a task requires action, but not right away. For example, you receive an email that says, "Here is the data. Send me the report when ready." Though no one asked you to start working then and there. You made it an immediate priority. Sometimes, you pick up an easy task just to pat yourself on the back for completing work. Whenever you are about to start a job, ask if it adds value and if you should work on it right now. Often, you have a better task, which isn't as comfortable to work on instead which yields better results.

Working on the wrong tasks leads to regret, long working hours, and a life of mediocrity. The worst consequence of poor prioritization is helping other people achieve their dream when you could spend the same time chasing yours. 2 seconds of mindfulness can help you spend time on what resonates with your heart and makes you happy in the long run.

Conclusion

Congratulations

So there you are, at the end of this book. Do you still believe 2 seconds are too short to make a difference? I hope not. You have learned how to make the most of two seconds in different aspects of your life. From here, all you need to do is starting using a pause before your decisions.

Like any other skill, you will forget to apply the 2-second principle when you begin. Let that not discourage you. After you keep reminding yourself for a week or two, you start questioning yourself automatically. You have to put in the effort to feed the pause into your subconscious.

Adapting to the skill is like learning driving. The first few times you are behind the steering wheel, you have to remind yourself to change gears, watch the mirror, and signal before taking a left. That's because you are driving using your conscious mind. Once you get the hang of driving, you no longer need to think about your hands and feet. They just what they have to because your subconscious mind knows what to do. But if you stop getting into the driver's seat because you haven't gotten accustomed, you will never learn to drive. Likewise, you will have to put in the effort to pause and evaluate before it turns into your default behavior. Once you get there, you will notice the difference it makes to your life and those around you.

Being more mindful with just a couple of extra seconds has changed my life. Sure, they haven't flashed me with million-dollar ideas, but they have helped me avoid countless mistakes. Once you put in the first few weeks of effort, you will reap the rewards for the rest of your life. After all, most of the good and bad in your life is a result of those little decisions you make every day. So, pause and get them right.

Before you leave, can you do me a favor please? If you found value from this book, please leave a short review on the platform. A longer one would be even better. Reviews are the easiest way to support the work of self-published authors.

The 2 minutes you spend on the review will be a great favor for me and make a lot of difference to help others find this book.

About the author

Maxim Dsouza is a personal development coach and a blogger. On his blog, Productive Club, he provides easy to follow actionable advice on:

- Time management and productivity
- Career growth
- Better decision making and critical thinking skills
- Entrepreneurship

He has spent over a decade experimenting and finding various time management techniques to improve his productivity. He strongly understands the fact that time is a limited commodity and tries to make every second count. He has extensive experience in leadership in startups, small businesses, and large corporations.

He has helped people of different professions and age groups gain clarity on their goals, improve focus, revise their time management skills, and develop an awareness of their psychological cognitive biases.

If you're keen on pursuing your dreams, improving yourself, or achieving personal growth, visit his blog Productive Club

His contact email is maxim_dsouza@productiveclub.com You can send an email to tell him that the book changed your life or wasted a few hours of your time. As per the rumors, he does not bite, so you reach out to him just to say hi if you like.